M000236904

"Cultural Brilliance is one of those rare books that stimulates the mind, inspires the heart, and offers tools for change. Claudette Rowley quickly gets to the heart of the matter: If you want a brilliant culture, you need to activate the greatness that's inherent in every organization."

—Barbara Huson (formerly Stanny),
author of *Secrets of Six-Figure Women*

"In *Cultural Brilliance: The DNA of Organizational Excellence*, Claudette Rowley presents a new narrative on culture that provides systematic guidance for the evolution of a brilliant, authentic successful organizational culture. An essential manual for twenty-first century organizations to enhance engagement and performance."

—David Krueger, MD, CEO of MentorPath,
and author of *The Secret Language of Money* (McGraw-Hill)

"*Cultural Brilliance* will help you build the business culture of your dreams! With creativity, imagination, and vision, this book helps organizations harness their potential for greater success. If you're looking for a new perspective on culture, a proven blueprint for change, and a dose of inspiration, pick up your copy of *Culture Brilliance* today."

—Kelly Sullivan Walden,
bestselling author of *It's All in Your Dreams*

"*Cultural Brilliance* gives leaders the steps and the mindset for aligning culture with strategy. If you want to bring out the best in your people, or simply become a better leader, this book is your guide."

—Marlene Chism,
author of *Stop Workplace Drama* and *No Drama Leadership*

"Whether you realize it or not, every action you take influences your company's culture, for better or worse, and that's true for every single person who works there. If you haven't put careful thought and serious effort into the culture you want to create—perhaps because there are always other things that seem more urgent—you should. Bad culture can bring down even a brilliant and powerful CEO, as it did at Uber. Good culture can help a company win the talent wars and then unleash that talent to create unprecedented innovation, as it does at Google.

"This book is a road map for creating an organizational culture that supports and empowers the people who work at your company, and thus your company itself. Rowley has drawn on her decades of experience to design a straightforward system for transforming culture, and provides real-world examples of how that system works."

—Minda Zetlin,
author, speaker, and "The Laid-Back Leader" columnist for *Inc.*

"*Cultural Brilliance* offers us a new road map for inclusive, intentional change that's driven, designed, and implemented by people at all levels of an organization. The Cultural Brilliance System allows the potential, invention, and intelligence of any workforce to emerge as it creates a culture that supports its growth and success."

—Doug Kirkpatrick,
keynote speaker, consultant, educator, and author of *Beyond Empowerment*, TEDx

"Every organization has a culture; is yours intentional or by default? Claudette Rowley offers a strengths-based approach that ignites innovation, productivity, and joy in the workplace by integrating curiosity, truth-telling, root cause analysis, and emotional awareness into the cultural norms. At all organizational levels, people become more comfortable with the uncomfortable, learning to trust one another, embracing change, and creating an inspiring culture."

—Rosemary Strunk, JD, GCSC,
Living Courageously, LLC

"In this insightful and practical book, Claudette Rowley shows the incredible power of workplace culture. But she doesn't stop there; she also provides a step-by-step road map for transforming your team or organization's culture into a catalyst for great performance, retention, and results. Recommended for leaders at all levels."

—Jocelyn Davis,
author of *The Greats on Leadership* and *The Art of Quiet Influence*

"We know that initiating and adapting to change can be a challenge for even the most growth-oriented companies. *Cultural Brilliance* offers us a new guidebook for respectful, authentic cultural change. By harnessing the power of mindset, systems, and co-creation, the Cultural Brilliance process motivates people to get clarity about their culture, design their vision for a better future, and put that design into successful practice."

—Hannah Ginley,
Chief People Officer for Windover Construction

"As humanity stands at a crossroads, Claudette Rowley shares why the business world is uniquely positioned to help us choose the path of human connection, dignity and abundance, and how by doing so we can create more profitable, innovative organizations. Her step-by-step system provides a road map to these outcomes, making it easier than ever to awaken the cultural brilliance in you and your organization."

— Samantha Thomas,
Founder and Director, Love Summit Business & Leadership
Conference and Just Choose Love

Cultural
Brilliance

Cultural Brilliance

The DNA of Organizational Excellence

Claudette Rowley

Waterside Publishing

Copyright ©2019 by Claudette Rowley

www.culturalbrilliance.com

All rights reserved. This book or any portion thereof
may not be reproduced or used in any manner whatsoever
without the express written permission of the publisher
except for the use of brief quotations in articles and book reviews.

Printed in the United States of America

First Printing, 2019

ISBN-13: 978-1-939116-57-4 print edition

ISBN-13: 978-1-943625-76-5 ebook edition

Waterside Press
2055 Oxford Ave
Cardiff, CA 92007

www.waterside.com

TABLE OF CONTENTS

*For Tim and Ethan
and
Dr. Pat Baccili*

INTRODUCTION

I was born believing in potential. I see potential in people, in organizations, and in society. I was also born with the ability to see reality clearly. This ability has set the foundation for my whole professional life: I can tell you where we are right now (the reality) and I can paint a vision for where we could be (the potential). But bridging this gap between current reality and future potential is my sweet spot. I created *Cultural Brilliance*™ because I believe we can do better as people, as organizations, and as a society to bridge the gap between our current reality and our potential. People who know me well often hear me say, "We know enough to solve virtually all the world's problems, but we don't do it. We have the intelligence, knowledge, technology, and capability to create a world that brings out the best in organizations and allows people to live in fairness, greater harmony, and opportunity." Why would we choose anything else? Yet every day, people and organizations choose a different path.

I believe that humanity is at a crossroads. Every day we hear stories of division, of disconnection from human kindness, and of people treating each other as though they don't matter. Every day we hear stories of positive action, of strangers reaching out to help each other, and of joy, kindness, and celebration. Every day we hear, read, and create both realities.

What do these dual realities have to do with culture, with business, and with brilliance? You might be thinking, "Isn't this a business book?" It most certainly is a business book, designed to help you create cultures that will enhance your business performance at every level of your company. Recognizing these dual realities is part of understanding corporate culture. I will deliver on my promise to you, to help you create cultural brilliance in your company, and more, but part of that requires recognizing the larger global context in which your company operates.

I wrote *Cultural Brilliance: The DNA of Organizational Excellence* because I believe the business world is uniquely positioned to help us choose the path of human connection, dignity, and abundance. This path doesn't sacrifice profitability, revenue generation, or innovation.

In fact, I believe that most businesses haven't reached their full profit potential because they are out of alignment with their people, their culture, and their ability to anticipate and implement change. What we know from quantum physics is that alignment matters. For example, the energy it takes to exploit your workforce to increase profits far outweighs the energy it would take to generate more revenue by respecting the people that work for you. As more businesses choose brilliance, respect, and kindness, the effect will be cumulative, changing the tenor of how we handle business within our world. Your organization's ability to pro-actively respond to change is a key factor in your strategy, innovation, and consciousness in the world economy.

Don't get me wrong; I love business strategy and making money. But business strategy and revenue can be generated from respect, adaptability, and conscious awareness—and learning this can be a key part of increased efficiency and better workplace culture.

For example, when you hold a team member accountable for his or her behavior, that can be an act of kindness. Each business that treats its workforce with respect increases the dignity in the world. When a business finds creative ways to reduce its carbon footprint, we can make the case that it's an act of brilliance. When a company creates a brilliant culture—an organizational system that proactively responds to change in ways that decrease stress, inspire learning, and promote organizational health—that's both an energetic and practical contribution to the rest of the world. Let me guide you through a cultural change system that has the power to revolutionize your business.

For the past twenty years, I have been honored to partner with and advise hundreds of leaders and organizations as an organizational development consultant and executive coach. In that time, I have learned a great deal about business culture. For instance, almost all of the companies I've worked with have struggled because their culture has been out of align-ment with their people, strategic objectives, and external environment. For instance, leaders in those companies would come together and dis-cuss ways to improve communication, resolve conflict, and make better decisions. Often working with great commitment, they tried to clarify expectations, improve problem-solving, and become more strategic.

Here's the thing, though: Although productivity and performance may have increased, the company usually still felt frustrated and stuck in a loop of mediocrity with an occasional spike of excellence. That's because at their root, they were trying to resolve cultural issues but didn't know it.

To use a metaphor, it's like putting a Band-Aid on a heavily bleeding wound—it's simply not going to staunch the flow. When culture constrains the organization's ability to move forward productively, the company is simply going to stall or get stuck, or, if it does move forward, it does so under great stress.

For years I have seen companies work around their cultural issues rather than confront them, avoid telling the truth about behavior, and over time, allow their culture to devolve, rather than evolve, into something nobody wanted. Often this occurs unintentionally, the result of corporate leadership not understanding how culture shapes the organization and how, simultaneously, the organization molds the culture.

Why would an organization create a culture it doesn't really want or create a culture that's pretty good but could be so much better? This is one of the key questions to understanding corporate culture, one of several we need to ask in evaluating the culture at our own companies.

I wrote this book to both help you explore these questions and give you practical applications, but more important, I wrote it because I believe that your company's culture can be brilliant.

While that brilliance will help you make more money and fulfill your organization's mission, it will also help you contribute to the world in vital ways. What follows are the three reasons *Cultural Brilliance* came to fruition; the first two address missing pieces in the collective narrative on culture and the last reason addresses the need for all of us to rise up and use our business power for the greater good.

1. Organizational culture thrives in truth.

2. You are always part of a company culture and your culture is constantly evolving, even at this moment. Culture is not something you can set aside; rather it is always present and needs to be respected accordingly.

3. You have an opportunity—and a responsibility—and I can help you rise to the occasion.

Organizational culture thrives in truth

As an organizational development consultant, I've witnessed amazing transformations when cultures begin to recognize and tell the truth about themselves. I've seen leaders in a family business who were barely speaking begin to communicate again, allowing them to implement positive, strategic changes that helped their culture evolve. I've witnessed educators begin addressing the power imbalance in their school once they discovered that their culture held an unconscious belief that conflict was wrong (which in turn created tremendous, unresolved conflict). As a culture consultant for an energy company, I've coached a leader who designed an organizational structure that allowed the brilliance, talent, and invention of several previously siloed departments to coalesce.

And unfortunately, I've also seen organizations shy away from telling the truth about their culture and stay stuck in mediocrity. This refusal to recognize and see the truth in turn continues to support tremendous inefficiency, which can cause talented people to leave at regular intervals.

You are always in a culture and your culture is evolving at this moment

You are always in a culture. Culture in your company isn't an "extra" you can sideline or otherwise avoid addressing until you have time. It isn't a chair you stick in the corner and ignore. Instead it's like standing in the middle of a swimming pool. Every minute of each day the culture in your organization is evolving and you are immersed in it.

When a company hires a new CEO, the cultural foundation shifts. When an organization decides to reorganize, the culture allows or constrains the success of the reorganization. When an engineering department of a software company decides to create a new product, the culture will influence the product development. If the product is a huge success, the culture will evolve and change accordingly.

Why is culture always evolving? Organizational culture operates as a system, and like most systems, it is in a continual state of evolution as new people, ideas, and decisions enter the system, and as people, processes, and old ideas exit the system.

Although I'll delve into this idea more fully in Chapter 2, here's a peek into what often happens in businesses: As they attempt to improve their culture, they reduce it to its more superficial elements or take a one-size-fits-all approach. In other words, businesses take action without understanding how making a change in one part of the culture will affect the rest of the system and may dilute the potential in other aspects of their culture.

For example, a leader may recognize that his teams are not getting along well after a reorganization and the resulting tension is slowing down productivity (a common problem). Instead of identifying the "glitches" in the organizational system, however, the leader organizes a series of social events that gloss over the relationship tensions. In fact, people may become more frustrated and say, "Ever since our company reorganized, people aren't getting along and everything takes twice as long to accomplish. Our CEO's response: Bring in lunch and dinner for us and organize a company outing. He's not even listening to us!"

Let me show how to make changes in your business culture that pave the way for growth and evolution.

You have an opportunity—and a responsibility—and I can help you rise to the occasion

I believe each business around the world can and should be doing more to recognize and act on three realities:

1. A business exists to do more than make money. Even if the primary function is to make a profit, the business impacts its workforce, the community in which it resides, and the larger society through its branding, products, and services.

2. A business influences the fabric of our larger culture, of our societal interactions, and the health of our planet. Take the iPhone, for example. Although only one product, it has changed the way we look at technology, communicate, and view the role of smartphones in our lives. Need I say more? Companies have an enormous impact on us in both positive and negative ways. Businesses like Apple have reshaped our communication, connection, what we value, and how we spend our time.

3. A business' workforce are social beings with a need to connect, to be treated with dignity and respect, and to develop their talents, skills, and competencies. I dislike the term "human capital." We are not human capital; we are human beings. Human capital allows employers to distance themselves from how they treat their workforce and turns them into "head counts" and "FTEs." Everyone who works for a business is a person.

How to use this book

Cultural Brilliance is a road map, a field guide, and a cultural treatise all-in-one. When addressing culture, organizations often focus on what is wrong, broken, or defective instead of what calls forth excellence in people. The Cultural Brilliance System™ reveals the hidden parts of the cultural "iceberg" through authentic involvement at all organizational levels, solutions that are co-designed by the workforce and leadership, and integration that moves beyond dialogue into iterative, systemic implementation. As you read this book, it will become clear that your company's facility with change and the ability to tap into your culture's potential are both competitive advantages.

This book is a journey and I'm your guide.

In Part One, we'll define and explore brilliant cultures. What are they? How do they develop? How do you maintain cultural brilliance? We'll learn the roles of authenticity, adaptogen design, and aware integration. I'll talk about how cultures lose their luster over time and common behavior dynamics and decisions that indicate that your culture isn't shining as much as it could be. Then together we will unravel how culture really is the DNA of your excellence. Finally, I'll share the keys to the cultural kingdom by teaching you how your culture operates as a system. Once you understand the systems approach, it is much easier to develop a brilliant culture.

You'll also meet the U.S.-based two companies who will accompany us through an application of the Cultural Brilliance System: Islington-Barrett, a utility company, and SN Controls, a manufacturing company, both based on the East Coast of the United States. Islington-Barrett, a seasoned company, supported individual growth and focused on creating a positive environment for the people that work there. As you'll read, the compliance department's culture had gotten stuck in a set of mindsets and behaviors that prevented key changes. SN Controls, on the other hand, had less experience discussing or addressing its culture. While this company was also considered an overall positive place to work, stress levels had increased sharply over the previous year. As the company intentionally grew, its systems and processes weren't able to adapt to the increased volume. As you'll read, we worked on finding the root cause of these issues and how their cultural systems were driving the stress and inefficiencies. Both the names of Islington-Barrett and SN Controls have been changed to protect their privacy. However, the insights, work products, and outcomes you'll read about are real and accurately reflect what these companies learned and how they evolved.

In Part Two, I'll guide you phase by phase through the Cultural Brilliance System. We'll explore each of the three phases in detail: Authenticity, Adaptogen Design, and Aware Integration. You'll leave each chapter with a thorough understanding of the phase, why it's important, and practical strategies, tools, and tips to implement in your organization. Additionally, we'll spend time on the brief, yet important transitions between each phase that are essential to your success: Contextual Emergence, Design Integrity, and Social Capital.

In Part Three, I'll describe the essential roles leaders play to develop and evolve brilliant cultures. Specifically, we'll delve into what makes leaders culturally brilliant and how leaders can see their culture more clearly, and how anyone can become a culture whisperer. I'll leave you with a checklist to help you stay on track, avoid common pitfalls, and harness the positive emotional energy in your culture.

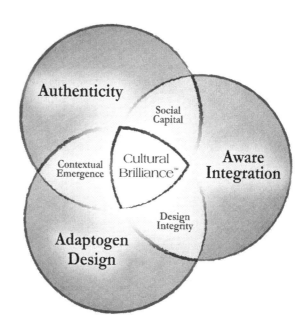

CULTURAL BRILLIANCE
SYSTEM: STEP-BY-STEP

Glossary

Throughout the book, we use terms that may be new to you. To ease understanding and simplify any complexity, a glossary has been compiled for your reference.

Adaptogen Design Phase: The second phase of the Cultural Brilliance System. During this phase, we create a design that articulates how your cultural system will functionally move from its current state to its future state.

Adaptogens: An adaptogen is a natural substance, such as an herbal medicine like ginseng or maca, considered to help the body adapt to stress and to exert a normalizing effect upon bodily processes.[1] The origins of "adaptogen" are the word *adapto* meaning "to adapt" and the suffix *gen* meaning "producing." As a result, an adaptogen is a system or entity that adapts and produces.

Authenticity Phase: The first phase of the Cultural Brilliance System. During this phase, we focus on determining how your cultural system functionally operates. We help you uncover the truth about your culture — how it's brilliant and how it blocks you.

Aware Integration Phase: The third phase of the Cultural Brilliance System. During this phase, we create a plan and then implement your cultural design.

Brilliant cultures: Organizational systems that proactively respond to change in ways that decrease stress, inspire learning, and promote organizational health.

Contextual Emergence transition: The transition between the Authenticity Phase and the Adaptogen Design Phase. During this transition, we develop a profile for your culture, including identifying your areas of brilliance as well as what blocks your organization.

Cultural intelligence: Your ability to see, hear, and understand the messages the cultural system is sending your organization.

Cultural systems: Mindsets, behaviors, and structures that sequence in often unseen patterns that drive organizational communication, decision-making, and results.

Design Integrity transition: The transition between the Adaptogen Design Phase and the Aware Integration Phase. During this transition, we prototype your cultural design in a team or department. Based on feedback, we refine the design before it's deployed throughout your organization.

Social Capital transition: The transition between Aware Integration and Authenticity. During this transition, we assess how your cultural systems have evolved and whether the original problem was solved. We also learn how your organization can stay brilliant.

The Cultural Brilliance System: Step-by-Step

AUTHENTICITY		
	To Be Accomplished	**Completed**
Step one	Set the stage for authentic cultural discovery	
Step two	Establish a Cultural Safety Zone	
Step three	Look your cultural elephant squarely in the eyes	
CONTEXTUAL EMERGENCE		
	To Be Accomplished	**Completed**
Step one	Harness the energies of transition, listening, and mindset	
Step two	Identify your cultural system's brilliance and blocks	
Step three	Develop a communication plan for optimal engagement	
ADAPTOGEN DESIGN		
	To Be Accomplished	**Completed**
Step one	Understand your individual role in change	
Step two	Learn the three-step Adaptogen Design process	
Step three	Decide how to apply and execute the design process	

DESIGN INTEGRITY		
	To Be Accomplished	**Completed**
Step one	Prototyping: Show, don't tell	
Step two	Design the feedback and check the logic	
Step three	Revisit the communication plan	
Step four	Identify growth and learning requirements	
AWARE INTEGRATION		
	To Be Accomplished	**Completed**
Step one	Plan preparation	
Step two	Develop your cultural integration plan	
Step three	Successful plan implementation	
SOCIAL CAPITAL		
	To Be Accomplished	**Completed**
Step one	Assess how your cultural system has evolved	
Step two	Learn how your cultural system stays brilliant	

Part One

The New Narrative on Culture

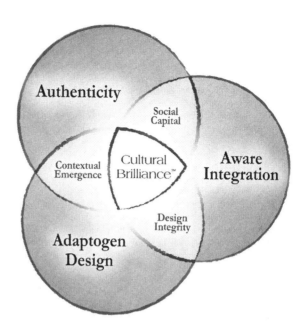

CHAPTER ONE

THE BRILLIANCE MANIFESTO

MOST BUSINESS CULTURES START OUT WITH A SPARK of new brilliance: A founder has an idea, a passion, a mission. From that spark a culture forms that initially meets the needs of its people, the systems, and their relationship to the external environment. As the organization grows, new ideas and people enter the cultural system, investors and customers develop specific expectations, and new business trends become popular. For many reasons, people can stop connecting with the original brilliance, disassociate from the cultural center, and begin to feel powerless to effect change. Despite brilliant beginnings, people can lose trust and faith in a business culture.

Good leaders will try to fix what's not working and often make situations worse by not first building solid trust with their people. Many times they

3

haven't yet created enough psychological safety—so even though their brilliant people have brilliant solutions to hard problems, they no longer feel safe to speak up in that culture. The culture itself can become ill and even toxic.

Formerly brilliant cultures that become unhealthy can be incredibly disappointing. Most people can tolerate some amount of cultural dysfunction and learn to work around it. But eventually, many people leave. Worse, some may adapt so much to the dysfunction that they get rewarded and promoted, unintentionally diminishing the culture in a downward spiral.

Does this sound familiar?

Most business cultures start out as brilliant. Some stay brilliant. Why? Because they listen to their people, build trust with their teams, and respond appropriately to the needs of the internal and external environments.

Imagine a brilliant culture that looks, sounds, and feels like this:

1. Respect, trust, truth, and psychological safety are the norm.

2. People are considered adults, not subordinates.

3. Peers take an interest in developing each other and giving constructive feedback.

4. Organizational purpose and direction are clear. People understand how they contribute to the larger whole.

5. Conflict is recast as productive and necessary for growth.

6. Problems are viewed as opportunities for expansion.

7. People understand how their culture guides their business.

8. Teams are self-managed and trusted to make decisions.

9. Leaders lead with integrity, self-awareness, and authenticity.

10. Productivity and innovation skyrocket as energy and inspiration spiral upward.

11. Change, competition, and external threats are viewed as opportunities to proactively adapt from a position of strength, positivity, and resilience.

Envision a culture that brings out the brilliance in people and that brilliance is reflected in the business strategy, problem-solving, and contribution to the greater good.

Now imagine that's *your* culture.

I believe in brilliant cultures. I believe that not only are they possible, they are necessary. Brilliant cultures lift people up. They are organizational systems that proactively respond to change in ways that decrease stress, inspire learning, and promote organizational health. Brilliant cultures adapt in a conscious state of change, are incisive, and make business-savvy decisions. They are responsive to the needs of their people, systems, and the external environment. Brilliant cultures recognize that if you don't get culture right and you don't get people right, you get very little right. In fact, I would question whether any business that treats its people unfairly or disrespectfully has ever reached its full potential as an enterprise.

This book is devised to teach you to create a more brilliant culture. Unfortunately, cultures can't move from dysfunctional to brilliant in one step — less healthy cultures may need some healing and repair first. My three-phase Cultural Brilliance System will help you discover the aspects of your culture that don't support your business strategy. Then by following the system, you'll learn how to design and implement a plan to create a culture that's aligned with your purpose, strategy, and goals. If you are forming a new corporate culture, this book will give you concepts, insights, and tools to start a brilliant one, and keep it that way.

In Part Two of the book, we move through each phase of the Cultural Brilliance System (Authenticity, Adaptogen Design, and Aware Integration) and teach you how to implement these phases in your organization.

But first, let's learn about brilliant cultures, why they really matter, and what dulls them.

What are brilliant cultures?

Let's define culture and take a detour to "culture school" for a few minutes. All organizations have a culture, which means that the people who make up the organization are in a culture, too. Often I find that people don't realize that they are *always* in a culture, similar to a vegetable being in a pot of soup. Even if people realize they are part of a culture, they frequently don't understand what that culture really is or that they can impact how it evolves. Edgar Schein, a forefather of organizational culture, defines culture as "a pattern of shared basic assumptions that a group learned as it solved its problems of external adaptation and internal integration".2 In other words, culture is a by-product of joint learning. Schein's definition speaks to the fact that culture is formed by the people in it. Although it's guided and influenced by organizational leaders, culture evolves daily as people communicate, solve problems, and make decisions. Tim Kuppler, Director of Culture and Organization Development with Human Synergistics and founder of CultureUniversity.com, explains culture as a system of shared values and beliefs that can lead to behavioral norms that guide the way people in an organization approach their work, interact with others, and solve problems.3 In addition to these definitions, it's helpful to keep in mind that organizational culture is neutral.

While we're defining culture, let's also define a few other key terms. In this book, we'll use the following definitions:

» **Brilliant culture:** Brilliant cultures are organizational systems that proactively respond to change in ways that decrease stress, inspire learning, and promote organizational health. We'll delve into this in far greater detail shortly.

» **Cultural intelligence:** Cultural intelligence is your ability to see, hear, and understand the messages the cultural system is sending your organization.

» **Cultural systems:** Mindsets, behaviors, and structures that sequence in often unseen patterns that drive organizational decision-making, communication, and results.

» **Organization:** Any group of people brought together for a purpose. In this book, we'll primarily be looking at corporate and small business examples, but the ideas can be adapted to any kind of organization.

When we refer to brilliance in cultures, we mean that these cultures reflect the intelligence, invention, and positivity of the people involved in them. In these cultures, we focus on what is right in people, their core central brilliance as they know it right now. Brilliant cultures harness the emotional intelligence of an organization. In these environments, people are aware of the potential inside of themselves and their culture. They connect seemingly disparate people, ideas, and processes to create something new, and the organization's purpose is congruent with who they are. Brilliant cultures bring out the best in people and those same people bring out the best in the culture.

Consider, for instance, Google's Project Aristotle, the project lens through which Google spent several years examining which traits led to team effectiveness. Prior to the study, Google, like many organizations, believed building great teams was simply a function of hiring great people. As Project Aristotle's leads Julia Rozovsky and Abeer Dubey noted, however, that isn't what Project Aristotle found.

Google's research team spent over two years studying 180 Google teams, which included conducting hundreds of interviews and analyzing 250 different team attributes. As they sifted through the data, they began to realize success was highly dependent on group norms—"the traditions, behavioral standards, and unwritten rules that govern how teams function when they gather . . . Norms can be unspoken or openly acknowledged, but their influence is often profound."[4]

In other words, performance was a function of culture. In particular, Rozovsky found five key characteristics that informed successful teams:

> » **Dependability.** This is the expectation that all team members will get things done on time and meet expectations.
> » **Structure and clarity.** The best-performing teams are made up of individuals who all have well-defined roles and work toward clear goals within those roles.
> » **Meaning.** The work holds significance to each person on the team, meaning they are personally invested in the work.

> » **Impact.** Each member of the team believes the work has purpose, and positively impacts the greater good.
>
> » **Psychological safety.** This proved to be the most important piece. Because each member of the team felt psychologically safe, they were able to take risks, share opinions, and ask judgment-free questions.

If that sounds a lot like brilliant culture, it's because it is.

The Google example also exemplifies how culture and the individuals within it have a symbiotic relationship. People evolve their culture as they work in it, make decisions, and learn together, and as the culture transforms, it influences how people interact. In brilliant cultures, this reciprocity is heightened by a level of cultural self-awareness: People possess insight about themselves, they understand how their organizational systems operate, and they "get" their culture at a deep level. They understand how their culture both helps them and hinders them, and they actively work to promote the culture's health. High trust, learning, and insight form the foundation of this cultural self-awareness. Neuroscience research supports this concept.

In his research on the neuroscience of trust, Paul J. Zak[5] found that creating a "culture of trust" is what has a lasting effect on long-term talent and retention. Zak was able to scientifically prove that trust increases oxytocin (one of the "feel good" hormones) in people's brains, therefore increasing our performance, engagement, and energy at work. Some of his more staggering statistics include that in high trust companies, employees display 74 percent less stress, 106 percent more energy at work, 50 percent more productivity, and 13 percent fewer sick days than people in other companies. Similarly, workers in high trust cultures were 76 percent more engaged and 29 percent more satisfied with their jobs and overall lives.

Unfortunately, in my work, I often see cultures suffering from the effects of low trust, cultures stuck on a treadmill of mediocrity, and cultures that keep getting in their own way. I work with companies that are close to breaking through to brilliance, but let it slip from their reach because they've enshrined cultural systems that are dysfunctional, inefficient, or breed mistrust. These cultures dull themselves and dim everything they touch, but especially the people within them.

A culture that has lost its luster will often make decisions without considering the impact of those decisions on its workforce. For example, when you remove office trash cans to avoid paying a cleaning service to empty them, what message are you sending to your team members? When a company announces a reorganization and doesn't give those impacted an opportunity to adjust and ask questions, it sends the message that those people don't matter. Time and time again, I witness managers unwilling to have crucial conversations at critical junctures. Often people do not receive the critical feedback that will trigger a change their behavior and then are demoted or laid off without warning. Without that feedback, the choice to change is stripped from them. At best, this approach is cowardly and at its worst, it's inhumane. Here's the bottom line, and something we will come back to throughout the book—**we can't change what we can't safely talk about.**

When cultures start to lack luster, I observe the following:

» Leaders don't give important, developmental feedback to their teams;

» People are afraid to tell the truth about their culture;

» Trust is so completely eroded that the culture has turned toxic and damaging to the people in it;

» There is a lack of emotional intelligence at all levels;

» People respond to change with intense resistance instead of curiosity;

» Leaders manage from a command and control perspective that no longer works and then wonder why people in their company won't innovate or are not open to trying new things;

» Organizations don't prioritize opportunities to learn from mistakes, failures, and missteps;

» People view new sales, customers, or ideas as "more work" rather than an opportunity to evolve;

» Business leaders forget that people are people, not human capital;

» Leaders are more concerned with defending their power than with leading;

> » Logic is replaced with short-term thinking about the bottom line; and
>
> » Leaders don't understand how culture and change work, despite the multitude of research on these topics.

The five signs that something needs to be fixed

If you are curious about where your culture stands, consider these five signs that your culture is not operating in a state of brilliance:

1. People are punished for telling the truth

In an emotionally safe, trusting organizational environment, telling the truth (as you see it) is encouraged. Sharing your perspective, thoughts, and ideas is considered vital to the success of the organization. In broken cultures, people lose jobs when they tell the truth, are marginalized when they don't toe the party line, or get passed over for a well-deserved promotion when they try to point out flaws in the current system. In short, truth-telling is met with an organizationally sanctioned punishment designed to keep people in their place. It's called the power of repression.

2. Leaders ask for more data and do nothing about the problem

This is often a disguise for "We really don't want to know anything or change anything. We hope that if we keep asking for data, you'll get tired and go away." If an organization asks for more data, it is incumbent upon the organization to act on the message in the data. When leaders ask for more data and don't respond proactively to the new information provided to them, they are communicating that they lack courage, are unwilling to confront reality, or are more concerned with maintaining their own power or comfort than they are with positively impacting their culture.

3. Your culture makes people leave

If your culture brings out the worst in people, your business most likely isn't doing well. You may have a revolving door as people recognize the truth, burn out, and depart. Usually these organizations are led by people who don't respect the workforce. These leaders may not care about people's individual engagement or success and haven't made creating a trusting environment a priority. Often, when people do succeed in these organizations, they do so by playing the political game to move ahead on the backs of others.

4. People work in an open space

On the surface, this doesn't sound like a big cultural issue. Here's the thing: In brilliant cultures, people get to work in accordance with their natural style and in alignment with their needs for space and connection. When an organization proclaims, "We will all work in an open space because then we will collaborate more," I often observe employees working with earbuds in their ears. Does collaboration really increase? Or are people "plugged in" so they can focus? I also notice that in many open space cultures, the environment is often silent. What if people enjoy the energy of connection, but can't get it unless they reserve a conference room? The truth is, for many companies open spaces, cubes, and other collaborative work space configurations aren't designed with work styles and needs in mind. Instead, open spaces allow a company to say it's collaborative while in practice often making work more challenging for some of its workforce.

5. Your culture tolerates bullying behavior

If your organization is tolerating bad, even bullying, behavior, you have a problem. Why do organizations tolerate bullies? In part, because they don't have strong boundaries around acceptable and unacceptable behavior. The culture may not have a track record of peer-to-peer accountability or expectations around behavioral norms. Perhaps senior leaders have held on to power themselves by bullying others. Often the excuse for not confronting a bully is something like, "He is a rainmaker. He brings in so much revenue or holds our largest account" or "She is technically brilliant. It would be so hard to replace her expertise."

It turns out that not only is there a cultural cost to allowing bullying behavior, there's also a financial cost to your organization.6 Begin by determining the time period during which the bully in question has been allowed to operate unchecked. Next, evaluate scope: How many people have been directly affected, in that they were targeted by the bully, or were aware of the bullying and indicated a desire to be away from the situation, either by quitting, transferring, or taking time off. Then evaluate turnover cost; a conservative estimate may be that replacing a worker costs 1.5 times their salary. Additionally, consider lost opportunity costs that arise when higher-contributing members of the team leave. Their exit may also mean losing their clients.

Trust me, everyone is replaceable, especially the bullies in your culture. Remember, a bully harnesses power by treating others badly and preying on their insecurities. Because a bully is aggressive and action-oriented, it's not surprising that they bring in revenue or contribute technically. Typically, these folks know how to get things done. Of course, they also typically increase the toxicity in your culture and drain its energy, all of which costs valuable time and money, and diminishes the overall health of the organization.

Creating a brilliant culture

In cultures that have lost their brilliance, people usually don't understand, at least not on a deep or meaningful level, how their cultures operate and how they unintentionally reinforce mindsets, behaviors, and decisions they don't want. For example, when people make mistakes in some cultures, they are publicly criticized. The leader offering the criticism justifies her behavior by telling herself she is sharing "constructive feedback." After someone is publicly chastised a few times, they usually shut down, do exactly what they believe the leader wants, and stop doing anything that resembles taking a risk. The leader may want to create a more innovative culture, but her behavior has helped the culture evolve into a risk-averse state, in turn stifling innovation.

In a brilliant culture, that scenario wouldn't occur, or if it did, it would be short-circuited quickly. If a leader publicly criticized a team member for making a mistake, that person would know he or she could stop the leader, share what he or she was experiencing, and request a different conversation. Brilliant cultures are authentic, and authentic cultures are built on trust, truth, and psychological safety.

These behaviors are constants in brilliant cultures:

» **Positive, complete communication**—A culture can't be responsive if its people aren't responsive to each other.

» **Psychological safety**—A climate of openness that develops when a group has "a shared belief that the team is safe for interpersonal risk taking."[7]

» **Inspired problem-solving**—People work to solve problems at the root cause, they understand how their solution will impact the larger system, and they seek to answer the question, "What's the solution no one has thought of yet?"

» **People walk their talk**—Organizational purpose and practice are aligned.

» **Balanced autonomy and collaboration**—People understand how their role fits into the larger picture. They know when to collaborate and when autonomy is the adaptable, productive response.

» **People are treated like adults**—They are fully functioning people who are able to make   important decisions and expected to successfully manage their own work lives.

Brilliant cultures operate in an interconnected system of Authenticity, Adaptogen Design, and Aware Integration. While we'll look at each of these phases of the Cultural Brilliance System in more detail in later chapters, let's briefly examine them now to help set the stage for what I want you to take from this book.

Authenticity is a willingness to tell the truth, develop an environment of psychological safety, and create a culture of positive, complete communication. In this first phase, we uncover the truth about a culture: what stops it from being brilliant. In Phase Two, Adaptogen Design, cultures are designed to proactively adapt to change in ways that decrease stress, inspire learning, and promote organizational health. In Aware Integration, Phase Three, companies plan and implement change with consciousness and intention. Not only are individuals in the organization self-aware, they are conscious of how their organizational systems operate, too. In a brilliant culture, Authenticity, Adaptogen Design, and Aware Integration all need to be active to illuminate the culture. One can't successfully exist without the other. Let's explore each one:

Authenticity

Jim and Julia sit down for a one-on-one meeting. Jim is Julia's manager and she has worked for him for three years at an automotive marketing company. During that time, she has been promoted twice into roles of increasing responsibility. Currently, Julia is the relationship manager on a $500,000 marketing account for a high-profile automotive company.

Recently, the automotive company started complaining about Julia—she's late for meetings, her communication has gotten spotty and unresponsive, and her ideas aren't as creative as they used to be. Jim is concerned and asked for this meeting with Julia.

Jim starts the conversation by outlining the information he's been given by the client, his concerns about the information, and the questions that the information prompts in his mind.

Julia listens closely, asks a few questions, and then shares with Jim what she has been experiencing with this client. Not surprisingly, her assessment of the situation is different. Julia tells Jim that the automotive company has given her a new contact, Nathan, and she's building a relationship with him. Interacting with Nathan has been demanding and time-consuming; he sends double the number of emails that his predecessor did and is highly critical of her ideas. She's been late for one meeting when she was stuck in a traffic jam.

Because Jim and Julia trust each other, Jim knows Julia is telling the truth and they start brainstorming the conversation they need to have with Nathan to reset boundaries, clarify expectations, and get to the bottom of his concerns.

In an authentic culture, it's that simple. There's no blaming, defensiveness, or mistrust. When mistakes are made, they are viewed as opportunities to learn. People tell the truth about themselves, their experiences, and the culture, and are encouraged to do so. This level of authenticity requires an acute ability to listen to oneself and other people. The culture is a "listening culture"; people understand the basic premise that, without active listening, communication can't take place in a productive way. My colleague, Terrie Lupberger, says that conversation is the basic unit of action in an organization.[8] Think about it: We do very little without communicating first, whether that is an email, phone call, or in-person conversation. In a brilliant culture, listening + conversation = one basic unit of action.

Without listening, asking questions from the perspective of curiosity, and fostering self-aware communication, we can't understand each other, make important decisions, and solve problems strategically. Authentic cultures embody emotional logic—what I call a logic-driven emotional intelligence. From this perspective, it's only logical that people are treated with respect, dignity, and trust, and that they are inspired to move forward in ways that push the edges of their brilliance. Looking through the lens of brilliance, treating people well is its own form of logic.

Authenticity requires a deep understanding of how the culture operates within an organization. As you think about Authenticity in your own company, consider the following questions as a guide, as your answers can help you evaluate and reevaluate as your company evolves:

> » What's it like to be in your culture?
> » Why does your organization exist? What's its purpose?
> » What's the tenor of the communication?
> » How does the culture help people grow?
> » How do people behave in the culture? What behaviors are rewarded, and what behaviors are tolerated?
> » How is conflict resolved?
> » How are decisions made and who makes them?
> » What does the organization value and believe? How are values and beliefs communicated?
> » What are the underlying cultural assumptions (unconscious beliefs that drive organizational behavior)?

Adaptogen Design

Brilliant cultures are organizational systems that proactively respond to change in ways that decrease stress, inspire learning, and promote organizational health. Instead of reacting to change from a state of resistance, stress, or fear, these cultures anticipate change, view it as normal, and recognize that all living entities thrive in a natural rhythm. Cultural design that's adaptogen in nature helps us achieve and maintain brilliance.

What do we mean by adaptogen? An adaptogen is a natural substance used in herbal medicine to normalize and regulate the systems of the body. Adaptogens help organisms adapt to environmental factors and avoid damage from these factors. When we examine the origin of the word, we find the Greek *adapto*, which means "to adjust" and the suffix *gen*, which means "producing." Adaptogens possess the properties of simultaneously adjusting and producing—an optimal combination for twenty-first-century cultures.

Adaptogen designed cultures relieve the stress of chaos, stuckness, frustration, feeling overwhelmed, or lost productivity by proactively anticipating and recognizing what's happening in the organizational ecosystem. Organizations recover faster and regain their energy in a new state of awareness, excellence, and inspiration. From an organizational perspective, an Adaptogen Design allows an organization to build up stores of strength, creativity, resilience, and brilliance.

An engineering company exemplified Adaptogen Design when redesigned the structure and workflow of its compliance department. In the original structure, the compliance team was charged with enforcing adherence to compliance standards, preparing for audits, and investigating compliance violations. No matter the volume, the work was shouldered by this team. Subject matter experts in each department had to comply with standards but did so as an afterthought. They believed that compliance was not part of their daily work; it was something extra to do.

After I facilitated a group cultural assessment, the director and I gained a deeper understanding of unmet needs, frustrations, and problems. Then a key team member informed her that he was applying for a new position within the company. The director stepped back and reflected on how what appeared to be a loss to the team could become a win for the company. After some thought, she had a breakthrough moment: What if the compliance department was redesigned as a more adaptogen structure? She replaced the single team structure with a new design that embedded a "compliance lead" in each department in the company. The compliance leads worked together proactively to solve company-wide problems. By meeting regularly, and as needed, they raised potential issues before they became problems. Rather than creating quick Band-Aid solutions, the compliance leads began addressing complex problems that had been draining company and individual energy for years, and when an urgent problem did surface, they were ready to handle it with inspiration and precision. The compliance leads became compliance leaders.

Aware Integration

Brilliant cultures evolve in a state of aware change. Not only do people have self-awareness, they have systems-awareness, too. (We'll explore this concept more fully in Chapter 2). As people communicate, they consciously tune into the culture and ask questions such as, "What do we need? What wants to emerge from the culture? As a organization, what are we learning?" But we can't function in a state of awareness without the ability to tell the truth about what we're experiencing, feeling, or observing. In aware cultures, the truth gets told.

Aware cultures view change as a form of learning and as a natural energetic state. From this perspective, change is not feared, avoided, or seen as an inconvenient obstacle. In fact, in brilliant cultures, a lack of change can be perceived as stagnation, and therefore, a possible cause for concern.

When cultures are authentic and adaptogen, they operate in a state of aware change. In less aware organizations, culture is not well understood, and even though it drives people's behavior, it remains an unseen influencer. People are often not conscious of the underlying cultural assumptions and beliefs.

For example, I facilitated a cultural assessment at a school. The staff and teachers were highly committed to their students and teaching philosophies. Yet they were having deep levels of unspoken, indirect conflict, which was stopping them from having important conversations about the growth and direction of the school. After assessing the culture, we discovered an underlying cultural belief that conflict was considered negative. One teacher articulated that, "If conflict is happening, something is definitely wrong." This unconscious belief was stopping the staff and teachers from engaging in meaningful conversations that included differing perspectives. As a result, their conversations were fractured and circular and, ironically, full of silent conflict.

Conversely, another culture might intentionally choose a belief that conflict is a natural part of discourse in a healthy organization. Because brilliant cultures build trust and psychological safety, strong differences of opinion are not viewed as risky. In fact, these differences are viewed as necessary for optimal organizational functioning. If an organization can't bring knowledge, data, or unpopular opinions to the surface, it cannot operate at the top of its game.

When an aware culture integrates change, these principles and perspectives are followed:

» The change is in the best interest of the overall organization.

» The introduction of the change is designed to create maximum inclusion, buy-in, and clarity for participants in the change.

» The change respects people and honors their dignity as human beings.

» People are asked what they need to know before the change begins.

» A robust communication plan, including feedback system, is initiated.

» People are acknowledged for their contributions, efforts, and individual brilliance.

» The change is consciously and intentionally designed.

Above all, process matters. An aware culture knows that the process by which we do something is almost as important as what we are doing. That level of intention sets the foundation for your success, growth, and health as a company. Now let's learn how aware, brilliant culture forms the DNA of your organization's excellence.

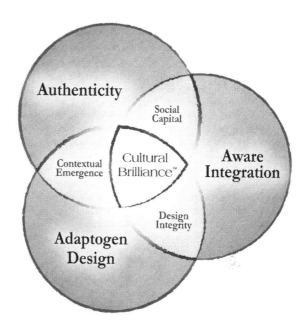

CHAPTER TWO

THE DNA OF ORGANIZATIONAL EXCELLENCE

WHAT WOULD IT TAKE TO BUILD A BRILLIANT CUL-
ture—a healthy organization that is innovative, courageous, and profitable?

You and your organization need to get in the game, into the mindset of possibility for your business. You need to understand that culture operates as a system and identify the beliefs, values, and assumptions driving your system's evolution. You need to be able to step outside your culture and observe it. How do people interact, communicate, and learn? Your enterprise evolves from the people, strategies, and decisions inside it, and the key to your success, historically and in the future, is locked within your organization's culture.

In *Leading from the Emerging Future: From Ego-System to Eco-System Economies*, C. Otto Scharmer says that "leadership is a distributed or collective capacity in a system, not just something that individuals do. Leadership is about the capacity of the whole system to sense and actualize the future that wants to emerge."[9]

What you are doing today sets the stage for your cultural tomorrow. That's good news and bad news. If you are intentional about how you develop your culture, then you will reap the benefits today and most certainly in the future. If you continue to allow your culture to evolve in ways detrimental to its brilliance, your company will most likely eventually falter.

Consider the example of the Philadelphia 76ers. For years, the Sixers were one of the worst teams in the NBA—even going so far as to intentionally trot out weak rosters in order to bolster their draft position. From that weakness and losing strategy, however, came a collection of gifted athletes, ultimately creating as promising a roster as any other team across the league. Under the leadership of Coach Brett Brown, the culture revived itself to be a formidable opponent within the NBA. As FanSided noted, "Even with a losing resume over the course of the past several seasons, Brett Brown has managed to scrape together a culture that supports belief." This is reflected in how the players support each other, cheering at one another's workouts.[10] This is culture trending upward, continually improving—and it's a perfect example of the kind of culture you want to create and foster in your organization.

Think about the cultural future that you want to emerge in your company. Will this future invoke brilliance? If not, you may want to consider a course correction.

It's long been stated that business culture drives business results. Peter Drucker is famous for saying that "culture eats strategy for breakfast." Edgar Schein expands on this idea by saying that business strategies will only work within the constraints of what a company's culture will allow.[11] In other words, if your strategy doesn't align with your culture, your culture will reject it.

Let's look at an analogy: When someone receives a lung transplant or a hip joint, their body may reject the new organ or new joint as a foreign body—something not recognized as part of the DNA of that particular person. Successful transplants or joint replacements require a process or a specific raw material, such as titanium, to convince the body to accept what's foreign. In other words, don't underestimate the power of your company's culture to thwart or support your business initiatives. Together, we'll look at examples throughout this book of how I've helped organizations recognize precisely the power of culture in their company, allowing them to harness that power for good.

To better understand how your culture can transform or bind your organization, let me guide you through a quick tutorial first—DNA and then systems thinking, and most important, how organizational culture operates.

What does DNA have to do with it?

DNA stands for deoxyribonucleic acid, which is the master molecule of every cell in the body. It contains vital information about individual biological traits that gets passed on to each successive generation of cells. DNA is also a metaphor that illuminates how cultural systems function.

From a 30,000-foot view, DNA replicates and adapts in a genetic system of relatedness. DNA doesn't exist in isolation, and in that way, culture is similar. As people get hired by an organization, work and contribute there, and leave, the culture evolves. Although culture doesn't replicate itself with the precision that DNA does, it evolves as a product of how people have interacted, what they've learned, and how they've made decisions. The culture itself carries the history of an organization and is a product of that history. In this sense, like DNA, culture communicates to successive generations and holds the power to drive or constrain organizational health and success. When a culture is brilliant, organizational excellence becomes part of your company's DNA.

Often, we see organizations reacting from the historical culture rather than identifying emerging needs, solutions, or paths, both in the present and the future. Organizations are held hostage by their culture only when they don't understand how the past influences the present. Unless strongly pushed by external forces, a company tends to respond to changes, ideas, and strategies through the lens of its culture.

Imagine that a corporation with management-driven emphasis on process acquires an innovative, technical company. The acquiring company, Peterson, Inc., has succeeded by creating a culture that focuses on process at the expense of long-term problem-solving. Peterson looks at each step of a process and refines that step to perfection. They manage the process by assigning a technical expert to each step. These technical experts do not necessarily communicate their changes to each other, making it a challenge for the process to operate as a system.

The acquired company, Hanson Brothers, has built its reputation on gathering the right people to solve the right problems. Due of its orientation toward the future, Hanson Brothers solves problems from a strategic perspective. This company employs a systems-thinking approach. When people solve problems, they seek to understand the underlying cause of the problem, as well as how the problem connects to the bigger picture. With the knowledge that they are in an evolving system, they try to solve the problem well enough, and then respond to the next challenge from a strategic perspective.

In this situation, there is a clash between a "drill down and refine to perfection for today" culture and a "let's understand, adapt, and problem solve for the future" culture. Is that a problem? It is if Peterson and Hanson Brothers don't understand their cultures and how they operate as very different systems. This knowledge is particularly crucial for Peterson, Inc. as the acquiring company. Because workforces are so steeped in their cultures, understanding their cultural beliefs and behaviors can be challenging. There is great value in teaching all organizational members how to become detached observers of their cultures. If they stand outside looking in, what will they see, hear, and learn? How can they create a culture that becomes the DNA of their own organizational excellence?

Culture is a system

In *The Fifth Discipline*, Peter Senge describes a system as the "key interrelationships that influence behavior over time."[12] These interrelationships are not only between people but also between variables such as resources, government policy, or emerging trends.

Simply put, a system is a group of consistently interacting people, concepts, or physical objects that form a unified whole. All systems are influenced by their environment and are part of other larger systems. For example, your company's cultural system incorporates many smaller systems:

1. How people communicate

2. How each department operates internally and cross-functionally

3. How the leadership team works

Your company is part of an even larger system: your industry, the natural environment, and the world economic system.

The ability to look through the lens of system is commonly referred to as systems thinking. Systems thinking is the perspective that we exist in webs or systems of interdependence. According to John Pourdehnad et al., "Systems thinking replaces reductionism (the belief that everything can be reduced to individual parts) with expansionism (the belief that a system is always a sub-system of some larger system), and analysis (gaining an understanding of the system by understanding its parts) with synthesis (explaining its role in the larger system of which it is a part)"[13]

Two useful examples of integrated systems are weather and the human body. Let's look at weather first. Weather functions as one large system impacting us locally in very different ways. Our local weather results from large global patterns in the atmosphere caused by the interactions of the sun, the ocean, diverse landscapes, and motion in space. What happens in one part of our weather system may create a significant weather event in another part of the world.

How about the human body? Since we each have a body, we have a ready-made opportunity to observe a system at work every minute of every day. We have a cardiovascular system, digestive system, nervous system, and immune system, to name a few, and each of these not only operates as their own system but they also enhance or impair the functioning of the other systems. The body itself is one large system encompassing many smaller systems. But when we go to seek medical treatment, what do we often experience? We may see a specialist who only looks through the lens of their area of expertise. How would our medical treatment change if a physician examined our whole physical system for patterns and was able to diagnose the symptom and the underlying root cause?

The same premise applies to culture. What happens in one part of a cultural system will reverberate throughout the entire culture. If a company lays off 10 percent of its workforce, the cultural system must adapt to the reduction of the workforce at three levels: the level of structure (environment, processes, and organizational design), the level of behavior (interaction, communication, decision-making, and execution), and the level of mindset (beliefs, values, mental models, and emotions).

> » At the level of structure, how will this 10 percent layoff impact the rest of the organizational system? At the very least, who will assume the responsibilities of the people who have been laid off?
>
> » At the level of behavior, how will the layoff change communication and decision-making systems? Were key decision makers included in the reduction? Are fewer people available to execute on critical priorities?
>
> » At the level of mindset, how do people feel about the workforce reduction? How was it explained to them? Were workers laid off respectfully? Do remaining employees have less trust in the company after the layoff? Or perhaps more trust because it was handled with care, respect, and dignity?

As Joseph Calitri, former director of Public Affairs at American Cyanamid Company, said in his speech *The Pursuit of Very Goodness*, "A systems approach . . . demands that each concerned part of the system must recognize the needs of every other part of the system and work to achieve a solution that will help all parts and the system as a whole."[14]

In *The Fifth Discipline*, Senge makes three points that directly and deeply influence organizational cultural systems:

Structure influences behavior

Different people in the same structure tend to produce qualitatively similar results. When there are problems, or performance fails to live up to what is intended, it is easy to find someone or something to blame. But, more often than we realize, systems cause their own crises, not external forces or individuals' mistakes.[15]

This is true for cultural systems as well. How often do we hear about a company's demise and, as we dig deeper, we find out that their strategic objectives were at cross-purposes to the organizational culture? In my work, I interact with leaders who are what I call "culture blind." These are leaders who don't understand how their culture operates, how it impacts success, stagnation, or failure, or how they, as a leader, impact the culture.

For example, I've interacted with leaders of start-up companies who were "blind" to how their culture was harming the morale, motivation, and ingenuity of their people. One company had a revolving door of people and was missing production deadlines because they couldn't keep pace with customer demands. The cultural system did not promote sustainable hiring or retention practices. In addition, no one in the culture was willing to tell the leader the truth about why they were missing deadlines. These two subsystems—hiring and retention, and organizational communication—caused their own crisis.

Structure in human systems is subtle

We tend to think of "structure" as external constraints on the individual. But, structure in complex living systems, such as the "structure" of the multiple "systems" in a human body (for example, the cardiovascular and neuromuscular) means the basic interrelationships that control behavior. In human systems, structure includes how people make decisions—the "operating policies" whereby we translate perceptions, goals, rules, and norms into actions.[16]

Using this same start-up as an example, the leader saw the symptom of the problem, the revolving door of employees, but couldn't necessarily see the basic interrelationships that caused that behavior. Early in the company's inception, decisions were made that created human systems that didn't work well. For example, when potential candidates were interviewed, the company took too long to make hiring decisions. By the time they contacted a candidate they wanted to hire, that person had taken another position. When people were hired, their pay was below industry standard. Once those workers learned their jobs well, acquired new skills, and felt more confident in their field, they would look for new, higher paying jobs.

Leverage often comes from new ways of thinking

In human systems, people often have potential leverage that they do not exercise because they focus only on their own decisions and ignore how their decisions affect others. [People] have it in their power to eliminate the extreme instabilities that invariably occur, but they fail to do so because they do not understand how they are creating the instability in the first place.[17]

In organizational culture, the mindsets that drive behavior are usually unknown. These mindsets influence patterns of behaviors that form in the culture, and quite often, people are not aware that these underlying cultural patterns exist. Even those who see these patterns of behaviors may be challenged to gain consensus from others in the larger cultural system.

As Senge says, "Systems of which we are unaware hold us prisoner." I say that systems of which we are aware and have the courage to discuss openly and change can set us free. Why does this matter? Your company may be trying to create a better culture, a brilliant culture, without understanding the systems in which you participate. Start to learn about your cultural systems. Draw them on a piece of paper, but not as an organizational chart. Instead, focus on how the systems really operate. Make a flow chart or use your own design. For example, map out how your operational, communication, or manufacturing systems operate and then note the behavior that causes each system to operate in that specific way. Finally, think through the mindsets driving the behavior. Make note of the larger systems your organization functions within. As we move through the Cultural Brilliance System, you'll be able to discern more about your company's systems.

Throughout the book, we'll refer to culture as a system. **Cultural systems are mindsets, behaviors, and structures that sequence in often unseen patterns that drive organizational communication, decision-making, and results.**

Six evolutions of a brilliant culture

The Cultural Brilliance System heals cultures that no longer work well, establishes road maps for cultures to stay brilliant, and helps new enterprises create brilliant cultures right from the beginning. But the Cultural Brilliance System does something else as well. It teaches individuals, teams, and leaders how cultures function, how they evolve, and to see them as systems. As an organization progresses through each evolution of the Cultural Brilliance System, people learn about their own culture, and, as a result, they can make conscious and intentional choices about how they want to guide it. This system is iterative as each success and insight builds on the previous one.

The Cultural Brilliance System is comprised of three phases: Authenticity, Adaptogen Design, and Aware Integration, and the three transitions between phases: Contextual Emergence, Design Integrity, and Social

Capital. In Part Two, we'll take a deep dive into each phase of the system and how these phases can be used in your business.

Authenticity: During this foundational phase, we uncover how your culture really operates. We use this information to identify specific cultural alignments and conflicts and then determine how they impact business success factors, organizational strategies, and team outcomes.

Contextual Emergence transition: We develop a cultural profile that identifies areas of brilliance as well as what blocks your organization. During this phase, organizational members offer vital feedback, ask questions, and help define the parameters of the culture change process. Simultaneously, we design and deploy a robust communication plan to update the workforce on next steps.

Adaptogen Design: Using design principles, we architect a brilliant culture for your organization. We determine how the culture will be expressed in areas such as leadership, communication, business outcomes, trust building, operations, structure, and environment. Based on this information, we design how the culture will move from what it was to a new form. How will people need to think and act differently to create a brilliant culture?

Design Integrity transition: Starting with one department or team, we test a prototype of your cultural design and ask for feedback on it. From there we leverage insights from the feedback and adjust the design.

Aware Integration: We develop and implement the cultural integration plan and deploy the next round of communication plans. The plan is implemented from the perspective of the new culture rather than the existing culture.

Social Capital transition: Through feedback and metrics, we determine how strategic objectives have been met, behaviors have changed, and engagement has increased. Has the culture evolved? Are problems being solved differently? Has business performance improved? Do people connect and relate differently?

Now that we've explored how brilliant cultures function as systems that form the DNA of your company's excellence, we'll turn our attention to deploying the Cultural Brilliance System in your organization. In the next chapter, we jump into the Authenticity Phase with both feet.

As you read the chapter, you'll want to think through the best ways to understand how your cultural system truly operates.

To give us an "on the ground" understanding of how you can use the process in your company, two companies will accompany us on our journey: Islington-Barrett, a utility company, and SN Controls, a manufacturing company, both based on the East Coast of the United States. Islington-Barrett, a seasoned company, supported individual growth and focused on creating a positive environment for the people that work there. As you'll read, the compliance department's culture had gotten stuck in a set of mindsets and behaviors that prevented key changes. SN Controls, on the other hand, had less experience discussing or addressing its culture. While this company was also considered an overall positive place to work, stress levels had increased sharply over the previous year. As the company intentionally grew, its systems and processes were unable to adapt to the increased volume. Both the names of Islington-Barrett and SN Controls have been changed to protect their privacy. However, the insights, work products, and outcomes you'll read about are real and accurately reflect what these companies learned and how they evolved. Both organizations used the Cultural Brilliance System to transform their cultural systems and ignite their brilliance. Let's learn how they did it.

Part Two

The Evolutions of a
Brilliant Culture

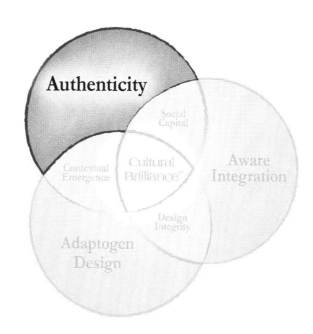

CHAPTER THREE

AUTHENTICITY PHASE: THE HEART OF CULTURE

ARE YOU WILLING TO TELL THE TRUTH ABOUT YOUR culture? This question is at the heart of cultural authenticity. By truth, I mean, are you willing to uncover how your culture operates in reality? Not how you hope it functions, how you've been led to believe it works, or what it says on your website. Truth includes the great and not-so-great parts of your culture—how it holds you back and moves you forward. What people love about it, tolerate about it, and hate about it. Understanding the authenticity of your culture also includes identifying the gaps between what we say we do and what we actually do. Seth Godin describes authenticity as "consistent emotional labor."[18] Do we react the same way when no one is looking?

You might be thinking, *Why would we want to open that can of worms?* We open it because we can't change what we don't fully understand. All too frequently leaders try to change a culture they haven't accurately assessed. As a Deloitte Human Capital Report in January 2016 notes, only 28 percent of survey respondents believe they understand their culture.[19] When we try to change what we don't understand, we usually end up with a big organizational mess on our hands. That's what we're trying to avoid when we uncover how culture authentically operates.

Authenticity is the first phase in the Cultural Brilliance System—whether building a new organizational culture, reworking a culture that's broken, or even transitioning a company from good to great. It's like a 360-degree review for your organization. Getting to the heart of authentic culture requires understanding how hidden and observable norms align, how safe people feel to tell the truth, and analyzing how habits, conflicts, and decisions are part of the cultural code—the unspoken "rules of engagement."[20] In a brilliant culture, people feel supported, are willing to be themselves, and can tell the truth about the culture and organization.

Cultural authenticity also honors the humanity of a culture by looking at the roles of belief and mindset. "Our beliefs are the software that drive our behavior," says Dr. David Krueger.[21] What we believe directly impacts our ability to build trust and to create the safe psychological space that's imperative for developing authentic culture. Throughout each phase of the Cultural Brilliance System, mindsets and beliefs plays a starring role. As we'll explore more deeply in this chapter, mindset, behavior, and structure are inextricably linked in cultural systems.

As we work through this process, we can't make assumptions about people and what they believe because doing so introduces the possibility of unnecessary fear, resistance, and unaccepted change. Instead, cultural changes require the full participation of everyone involved. As a result, developing authentic culture may require sending out a search party for resistance by asking the tough questions and really hearing the answers—then getting to the emotional heart behind the resistance.

The good news is the skills, insights, and strategies needed to uncover your culture's authenticity are the same ones needed for your culture to maintain its authenticity.

In this chapter, we'll focus on the three steps you need to complete in the Authenticity Phase:

Step One: Set the stage for authentic cultural discovery
Step Two: Establish a Cultural Safety Zone
Step Three: Look your cultural elephant squarely in the eyes

▶ **STEP ONE:**
Set the stage for authentic cultural discovery

Before we dig in and excavate how your culture really operates, we need to put up some scaffolding to guide the process in the best direction. Fortunately, this is not difficult to do, and the effort you put into this phase of the project will pay off in spades. As you begin to engage in the Authenticity Phase of the Cultural Brilliance System, you have a few items to consider:

> » How will you introduce the Cultural Brilliance System to your organization? You won't want to send an email announcement and call it good, for example. You will want to organize in-person and virtual town hall meetings to answer three key questions: Why do we need to design a cultural change? What are we planning to accomplish? What will people's involvement be throughout the process? You'll want to leave plenty of room for questions, feedback, and concerns.
>
> » What is the cultural problem you are trying to solve? There's a reason you are embarking on this journey. Let's be conscious and intentional about why. You might decide your culture needs a reboot because it no longer supports your strategic objectives. To keep pace with the competition, you may need to accelerate innovation and your culture isn't innovative. You may have a low trust culture that's holding you back from your potential. Whatever the answer is, just make sure you tell the absolute truth about what you intend to accomplish.
>
> » How will you communicate and get feedback during this cultural evolution process? This question is a more practical one. You'll want to look at existing communication and feedback vehicles within your company and harness those.

> Depending on your size, you may want to create online communication opportunities for people to leave questions, offer feedback, or engage in discussion.

These are important questions for you to answer, whether you're the CEO of a $100 million corporation or the leader of a ten-person team in a VC-funded start-up. As I'll say several times throughout this book: *How we design the introduction of a change process is almost as important as the change process itself.* Introductions matter. If you gloss over the introduction of the Authenticity Phase and assume everyone will fall into line, you will almost certainly generate unnecessary resistance.

When I begin guiding an organization through the Cultural Brilliance System, I often lead interactive sessions on two important topics: 1.) Listen to what you hear and practice the art of curiosity, and 2.) How to understand cultural systems and intelligence.

I'll share the key concepts here to help you jump-start your organizational journey into cultural brilliance.

Listen to what you hear and practice the art of curiosity

Why do I prepare an organization to uncover its authentic culture by discussing listening? Because listening is one of the keys to a brilliant culture. If we can't listen, we can't communicate, we can't self-reflect, and we can't strategize. Listening is also the basis of empathy, design, growth, and learning. As we'll discuss in Chapter 9, listening is a foundation of culturally brilliant leadership. Listening is not only allowing words to enter your ears and then your brain. Listening closely is a form of respect and connection. Good listening communicates, "I hear you and acknowledge you. What you have to say is important."

If listening is the call, then asking good questions is the response. Perhaps you've heard someone say there's no such thing as a bad question. That's not entirely true. But there is no such thing as a bad *authentic* question. If you're not exercising the art of curiosity, it's difficult to ask authentic questions.

Authentic questions are rooted in curiosity, and curiosity sits at the center of good communication. Consider different types of questions you might hear in any of your company's meetings: How many of those questions are rooted in curiosity (and the genuine desire to know something), and how many of them are instead questions disguised as a way to showcase the speaker's own viewpoints (such as rhetorical or leading questions)?

In many organizations, conversations de-emphasize listening. Instead of asking curious questions, managers ask leading questions. And as Edgar Schein emphasizes in his book *Humble Inquiry: The Gentle Art of Asking Instead of Telling*,[22] that just won't do when it comes to building a healthy organizational culture.

As Schein notes, humble inquiry is "the skill and the art of drawing someone out, of asking questions to which you do not already know the answer, of building a relationship based on curiosity and interest in the other person."

How many people in your organization practice humble inquiry?

In most organizations, very few. And that makes sense. As Schein adds, many of us have grown accustomed to questions that tell, rather than ask: "leading questions, rhetorical questions, embarrassing questions, or statements in the form of questions—such as journalists seem to love—which are deliberately provocative and intended to put you down."

Those aren't questions that set the stage for a cultural system to thrive.

"We fail to notice how often even our questions are just another form of telling—rhetorical or just testing whether what we think is right." Schein adds, "We are biased toward telling instead of asking because we live in a pragmatic, problem-solving culture in which knowing things and telling others what we know is valued."

Asking ourselves questions rooted in curiosity is just as important as asking other people. To cope with stress, changes, or fear, we may not listen to ourselves very well. To create a brilliant culture, though, we need to do the exact opposite: We need to tune back into ourselves. What do we think? How do we feel? What's our intuition telling us about a situation? What's the elephant in the room no one is willing to discuss? If we're so busy, frantic, and overloaded that we are numb to personal interactions and to ourselves, how can we sense when something unspoken changes or there's an obvious problem?

How to understand cultural systems and intelligence

As we learned in Chapter 2, culture operates as a system.

When we look at culture through the lens of a system, we can see it more easily, discern why certain projects get stuck, and why some teams succeed and others don't. Culture isn't just about "how we do things around here"—it's a deep dive into understanding how organizational beliefs and assumptions drive daily behavior. These organizational beliefs and assumptions are, in turn, fueled by the historical DNA of your organization and create your cultural system. A cultural system is mindsets, behaviors, and structures that sequence in often unseen patterns that drive organizational decision-making, communication, and results.

For example, your company's cultural system incorporates many smaller systems—subsystems or subcultures—including how people communicate, how each department operates internally and cross-functionally, and how the leadership team works. Similarly, your company is part of an even larger system, made up of your industry, the environment your company impacts, and the world economic system. Thinking in systems can help us understand the relationships between those systems.

Appreciating the interplay of those systems helps us discover how your culture authentically operates at three levels: the level of mindset (belief, values, mental models, and emotions), the level of behavior (interaction, communication, decision-making, and execution), and the level of structure (environment, processes, and organizational design).

Some organizations do a better job than others of addressing all three levels. And when organizations fail to bridge those levels, the consequences can be dire. In some organizations, that level of miscommunication and organizational disarray can lead to tragedies. At NASA, for instance, organizational disconnectedness and the failure to bridge subsystems within the organization have contributed to several tragedies that cost lives, including the Columbia and Challenger failures. Let's explore one example noting the interplay of mindset, behavior, and structure.

As Henry Petroski, a civil engineer at Duke University, noted after the 2003 space shuttle Columbia failure,[23] the loss could have been avoided had the organizational structure been more sound (structure) and the people involved been more openly communicative (behavior). Instead, the organizational culture was such that only managers prevailed in the decision-making process (mindset and behavior), leaving the scientists and engineers unheard.

Had scientists and engineers truly had a seat at the decision-making table, and their input been properly valued, it is quite possible that both disasters might have been avoided. Instead, managers existed in a culture that devalued the expertise scientists and engineers brought to the table, and that broken cultural system resulted in the loss of life.

Because managers devalued others' expertise to overvalue their own importance (mindset), key pieces of information were lost (behavior). In the case of the Challenger explosion, an O-ring that wasn't designed for such cold conditions failed—a wholly avoidable mistake had engineers' warnings been heard and improved testing been offered/allowed (structure). Indeed, the official Rogers report commissioned after the accident found that, not only had NASA known for six years prior that the O-rings had issues (mindset, behavior, and structure), but also that organizational dysfunction was a root cause of the disaster.[24] Just as before, the investigation found that a breakdown in the cultural system was a root cause of otherwise preventable catastrophes.[25]

Reviewing this interplay of mindset, behavior, and structure can also help you understand the concept of cultural intelligence. Simply put, cultural intelligence is your ability to understand, see, and hear the messages the cultural system is sending your organization. When we employ our cultural intelligence, we become keen observers of systems, of how people interact, and the spoken and unspoken messaging moving through a company.

For example, cultural intelligence played a big role when I worked with a successful family business in the restaurant industry. Although the business had been purchased by two family members and a longtime organizational leader, the founder still held sway over the company. The new owners wanted to assume operational leadership of the company, but the founder was having difficulty letting go of power and authority. Each of the three new owners used their cultural intelligence to tune into the complex organizational dynamics. Although initially they were struggling to communicate with each other, they each independently assessed the cultural issues accurately. Once the three owners realized that they were fundamentally aligned, they were able to communicate more effectively. Eventually, they were also able to ask the founder to step back from daily involvement with the business. Each of the three new owners assumed operational control in their areas of expertise and began to revamp the business and the culture, leading it to its next level of success.

For a practical application, here's an exercise from CRR Global I often use with teams to help them begin to hone their cultural intelligence—their ability to understand, see, and hear the messages the cultural system is sending to their organization. People break into small groups and *only* ask questions about upcoming change or uncertainty. We use "what if" questions to get started. For example, "What if we lose the positivity in our culture?" "What if I don't like working here anymore?" "What if we change too much and things get worse?" As groups keep asking questions, their old stories (which are based in beliefs, norms, and values) about their culture, a change, or other concerns start to lose their hold, and they begin to see new possibilities. Old stories about our organization, our culture, or ourselves tend to block our ability to see things differently. When we can listen to what is beneath the surface of the stories, we can more clearly access our cultural intelligence.[26]

▶ STEP TWO:
Establish a Cultural Safety Zone

As a cultural consultant, I work with my organizational clients to create safe enough spaces for open and honest conversations during all three phases of the Cultural Brilliance System. Trust, psychological safety, and truth form a cornerstone of brilliant cultures. Why? *Without an intentionally safe environment, how can we ask people to tell the good, the bad, and the ugly about their culture when it's a system they need to spend time in every day?* How can we design systems that proactively respond to change in ways that decrease stress, inspire learning, and promote organizational health if people are concerned about potential retaliation and betrayal by others?

Harvard Business School Professor Amy Edmondson's research on high performing teams in the late 1990s yielded the groundbreaking concept of psychological safety. According to Edmondson, psychological safety is a "belief that one will not be punished or humiliated for speaking up with ideas, questions, concerns, or mistakes."[27] Edmondson found that teams that made mistakes were more successful than other teams when they took the time to discuss and learn from their mistakes. This knowledge exchange opened the door to greater innovation, curiosity, and emotional risk-taking. Creating an environment in which people feel comfortable to take risks is key to fostering innovative workplaces.[28]

And neuroscience supports this. As neuroscience researcher Paul J. Zak[29] notes, creating a "culture of trust" is what allows organizations with a thriving culture to develop long-term talent and retain their best people. As referenced in Chapter 1, Zak's research shows that trust increases oxytocin, one of the hormones that makes us feel good, and that in turn makes us better contributors because our performance, engagement, and energy all increase as a result. And this has tangible economic benefits, as his previous research clearly demonstrated.[30] In particular, Zak identifies eight management behaviors that are especially important for organizations hoping to foster trust, and additionally may promote innovation as individuals try different approaches and naturally come upon more radically efficient ideas. Among those eight are the following four[31]:

1. Allow individuals to choose their projects.

When organizations allow their people to self-organize their own work groups, they feel trusted and take greater ownership because they're being allowed to invest their energies on projects they're already passionate about. It's still important that clear expectations are set and evaluations remain part of the conclusion of any project, but allowing employees to follow their passions understandably helps them feel more valued and greatly affects workplace culture.

2. Clearly communicate information.

This also means sharing that information broadly. Transparency is a sign of trust, and ongoing, open communication translates to business success,[32] and Google's research supports it.[33] When team members socialize and connect with each other, performance improves. When employees connect with each other, they feel supported. Additionally, they may be more likely to gain others' respect as well as to add respect for others, leading to a more driven workforce. When people care about each other, they are more likely to help each other with work projects, just as they are more likely to ask for help when they need it.

3. Encourage personal development.

When people work in high-trust environments where they feel like they grow as people, they are more invested in their work. Work-life integration and room for personal lives are an important part of helping everyone feel valued, and they contribute to engagement and retention.

4. Allow vulnerability.

That means encouraging team members to ask for help when they need it. When workplaces expect everyone to be able to do everything without ever needing help, it creates an environment that can be toxic and unrealistic. When workplaces provide support and make it easy to ask for help, performance improves. And this can come directly from the top; when leaders are willing to ask for help from their employees, it shows that they are more secure in their position of leadership and that they value what their teams can add, both of which help improve trust.

Unfortunately, many organizations either don't value these high-trust behaviors or, if they value them, don't know how to operationalize them, and as a result, everyone suffers. Developing a trusting environment starts with open conversation. We can't change what we can't talk about, which is another reason to establish a Cultural Safety Zone.

How to create a Cultural Safety Zone

1. Raise the question. What would make it as safe and comfortable as possible for us to discuss our culture? Discuss the idea of a Cultural Safety Zone—a "container," so to speak, for honest and open conversations about how your culture really operates, including the good, the bad, and the ugly.

2. Present the concept of psychological safety (as described above). Discuss what trust and psychological safety would look like in your organization. Even if everyone agrees that your workplace is not psychologically safe right now, talking about what psychological safety would look and sound like at your company sets the stage for that possibility to emerge.

3. Generate a list of ground rules or "guardrails" for your discussions. These lists often include *respect, honesty, open participation,*

a willingness to hear different viewpoints, confidentiality, no judgment, one person talks at a time, and it's okay to not know. There may be items on your list that are specific to your organization and may not exist on any other lists. The act of creating the list often evokes a higher level of emotional safety for many people. Be sure to bring the list to all cultural discussions and hang it on the wall. If you're having a digital conversation, be sure to reference the ground rules.

4. People from all levels and departments of your organization need to be involved in this process. This is one key for buy-in, motivation, and accuracy during the Authenticity Phase. Inclusion also builds safety. When we know that our voices will be heard, we are more likely to engage in the level of vulnerability required for telling the truth.

5. If you need to, bring in a neutral third party facilitator. A neutral third party can often be viewed as a safety net in case tensions rise or people don't feel heard.

First note: You don't need a high level of trust, or even much trust at all, in your culture to begin to have open and honest conversations about it. Throughout the Authenticity Phase, trust and safety begin to build as people get to assess, express, and tell the truth about their culture experiences. The exercises that follow are designed to keep the focus on your culture, not on individual people, teams, or departments. The goal is to look at how your cultural system, as a whole, operates.

Second note: Even when you do the very best you can to create a Cultural Safety Zone, it's not uncommon for the dysfunction in the existing culture to show up temporarily in people's behavior, especially once you begin to implement your plans for cultural change (covered in Chapters 6 and 7). If you're tempted to skip or to give short shrift to the development of the Cultural Safety Zone, please rethink that temptation. What is not working in your cultural system will rise to the surface to be seen and may temporarily increase stress, anxiety, or uncertainty.

▶ **STEP THREE:**
Look your cultural elephant squarely in the eyes

Step three of the Authenticity Phase outlines options for uncovering how your culture authentically operates. The goal is to excavate information people are not consciously aware of or don't speak openly about. The goal is to name what's *really* holding you back and identify your roadblocks and your brilliance. During step three, it's important to refrain from making judgments or assumptions about what you'll uncover about your culture. After facilitating the Cultural Brilliance System many times, I'm always surprised by what an organization discovers. This speaks to the unique nature of cultural systems. Just like a fingerprint, no two are exactly alike.

The goal is not for someone, such as a consultant, external facilitator, or executive level leader to tell everyone the culture they have. The goal is to pave the way for the people in the organization to discover the inner workings of their own culture. It's easier for people to consider, accept, and change what they have themselves authentically uncovered.

Let's start with a quick refresher on cultural systems and the three levels of culture

Cultural systems are mindsets, behaviors, and structures that sequence in (often unseen) patterns that drive organizational decision-making, communication, and results. As a result, culture evolves on a daily basis as people interact with each other and the outside world. As these systems evolve, they don't take into account accuracy or truth. Evolution is simply based on what is being learned, consciously or unconsciously, by the people in the culture.

According to Edgar Schein,[34] culture operates at three descending levels, which is one of the reasons it can appear nebulous and may be hard to wrap our collective heads around.

> » **Artifacts.** Aspects of the culture you see and feel. Artifacts include the physical items, such as the appearance of your office or grounds. Behavior is also an artifact because we can observe it. Behavior includes how meetings are run, how conflicts are handled, and anything we can see people doing. The energy or "vibe" of your company is also an artifact. What does feel like to be at work? Is there tension? Is it draining? Is it exciting or peaceful?

> » **Espoused Values.** These are the values that are commonly known throughout your organization. They may be listed on your website or in other literature. They may be known but rarely discussed. They may also be "official" company values that aren't honored very often. Respect, integrity, creativity, excellence, and efficiency are all common values.
>
> » **Underlying Assumptions.** Unconscious, taken for granted beliefs that drive perception, behavior, thought, and feeling in an organizational culture. These assumptions can both help or hinder the culture. We'll learn more about unconscious assumptions when we review the Culture Assessment Process later in this chapter.

Keep these three levels in mind as you assess your company.

Next, we'll review examples of assessments, tools, and processes you can use to get to the heart of your culture, understand how your cultural systems function, and reveal key cultural artifacts, beliefs, and assumptions. We want to think about uncovering this information as a two-step process: discover and assess.

Discovery Interviews

Once I complete steps one and two of the Authenticity Phase, I will often organize 20- or 30-minute confidential interviews with people at all levels and departments throughout the organization. Depending on the size of the company, I'll interview between 10-50 people. The goal is two-fold: to build trust and to discover. During these conversations, I learn a tremendous amount about what's important to people, what they want, and what's missing. These discussions also help to ease people into talking about their culture and normalize their emotional responses. You'll want to gather as many perspectives as possible—from the front line up to top leadership. I tailor these questions to the organization and will generally select five to seven questions depending on the goals of the cultural change. In your company, you'll want to select one to three people who are trusted and well-suited to assume the role of neutral interviewer. You'll want to make it very clear that the interviews are confidential; you'll also want to clarify how the interview information will be used.

My three go-to questions are

1. What are the bright spots in your culture?

2. What are the points of tension? (This tension could be between people or within a system or process.)

3. If I gave you a magic wand, what three changes would you make? (You'd have the power, authority, and resources to make these changes.)

A sample list of other relevant questions include

1. What are people talking about in your organization? How are they talking about it?

2. What's the emotional culture? What are people allowed to express? What gets suppressed?

3. What behaviors are tolerated? What behaviors get rewarded?

4. How are decisions made? Who makes them and how?

5. How is trust built? How would you describe the level of trust?

6. How is conflict handled? What types of conflict do you observe?

7. What are barriers to collaboration?

8. How do people relate and connect? According to the organization chart? Or in other ways?

9. Are there silos? Do certain people, teams, or departments act as bridges or interpreters for other teams or departments?

Typically, I will compile the interview data into a list that identifies themes, trends, and patterns and send it back to the organization for review. Inputting the data into Survey Monkey or a similar platform is another option, especially if you've interviewed more than fifteen people. You'll have an opportunity to represent the qualitative data graphically and to organize reports from different perspectives. *As you compile the data, you want to watch for trends and themes. What are people consistently mentioning? What is no one mentioning? What's emerging as an area to further explore?*

CultureTalk: A human framework

One tool I use for conducting a culture assessment is the ***CultureTalk™ Survey System.***[35] CultureTalk is an online survey that defines *organizational culture* through storylines called archetypes. Cynthia Forstmann, Theresa Agresta, and Andrea Cotter, founders of CultureTalk, offer organizations a unique perspective on how their cultural systems operate by identifying twelve behavioral patterns. An inherent aspect of authenticity is the acknowledgment that there is no "perfect" culture, rather we need to uncover and own both our organizational strengths as well as behaviors that are standing in the way of our progress.

Archetyping is a concept that was first introduced by the Swiss psychologist Carl G. Jung in his study of the unconscious energies that influence human behavior. He used the term *archetypes* to describe those deeper human stories that are universally recognized and to allow us to make sense of our experiences.

Consider the twelve archetypes of CultureTalk. Just scanning the list, I bet you can already guess what each of these storylines is about. Heroes save the day. Magicians transform. Revolutionaries break boundaries.

Now, take a moment and think about which archetypes might be part of your own story . . . or your organization's story. Can you just as quickly rule out archetypes that are not part of your culture?

One reason the archetypes work so well in defining culture is that they are human stories; they are rich and colorful but also flawed and relatable. We can use them both to position our strengths and to identify our shadow traits and opportunities for growth.

CultureTalk provides a quick way get everyone on the same page about their culture and the archetypes provide a shortcut to understanding and a language for talking about culture in a meaningful way. Although I've found this survey to be useful in many companies, I find it particularly helpful when an organization hasn't spent much time discussing or working on its culture.

When SN Controls team members took the CultureTalk Survey, their three top archetypes were the Hero, the Innocent, and the Ruler. The Hero is a "firefighter" archetype, willing to do whatever it takes to get the job done. The Innocent is trustworthy and accepting, with high integrity. The Ruler archetype has authority to create and enforce necessary rules, policies, and procedures. Below we see a breakout of SN Controls' archetypal strengths and shadows. The lists were generated by SN Controls team members when we validated their results.

Archetype Strengths

HERO	INNOCENT	RULER
Drop everything to meet customer's needs	Potential customers always become customers after touring facility	Ship as scheduled
Make sure product gets shipped	Gain trust when we ship early or on time to customers	Get things done right the first time
Get difficult customers what they want	Flexible with employees	Follow through on documents and processes
Get things done, on time, almost every time	Confident that a process will work the first time	Make sure product has passed quality control inspection
Teamwork	Care and happiness for employees—a family company	Follow processes
Learn new processes	Customers trust what we convey	Trust leader and the process
Do our best to make it happen		Obey and follow company's rules and regulations at all times with no excuses

Archetype Shadows

HERO	INNOCENT	RULER
Put work ahead of personal life	Bite off more than we can chew—put sale ahead of planning	Wrong product to wrong customer due to volume and capacity
Burn out	A new method of training is needed	Sometimes clash with each other due to miscommunication or no communication
Reactionary	Employees are stressed	Customer complaints because too much scheduled for limited capacity
Mistakes get made	Only some employees step up	Decisions made in a vacuum
Bail out customer but take the hit internally	No plan B	Use old processes
Work too long under stressful conditions	Can't think how to improve things when caught up in daily tasks	Rude to coworkers
Work long hours, skip lunch, work holidays		Vendors give excuses
Blame and finger-point		Need to communicate and plan proactively
Ineffective communication		Process first, people second

HERO	INNOCENT	RULER
Not know if the part we make meets specifications		Obey and follow company's rules and regulations at all times with no excuses
Employees genuinely feel bad for their mistakes		
Need planning and communication when material arrives		
No time for proper training		
Deal with inferior quality		
No cross-training		

Culture assessment process

In his book, *Organizational Culture and Leadership*, Edgar Schein[36] outlines a facilitated culture assessment process called "Rapid Deciphering—A Multistep Group Process". I run Dr. Schein's process with almost every organization during the Authenticity Phase. It uncovers underlying cultural assumptions brilliantly and helps to build a common language around culture. As Dr. Schein says,[37] "Culture is a set of shared assumptions...the contextual meaning of cultural assumptions can only be fully understood by members of the culture." As a result, creating an opportunity for people to understand their organization's cultural assumptions is an important part of the Authenticity Phase.

What follows is how I used the culture assessment process with Islington-Barrett, the utility company that had heavy compliance requirements. In this company, compliance was viewed as a "burden" and was usually approached in a reactive, versus a proactive, manner. The Director of Compliance wanted to shift the culture of compliance from being viewed as a burden to an opportunity for innovation and strategic, proactive planning.

This group assessment process requires a half day and should be facilitated by either an outside facilitator or a leader external to your team or department to ensure neutrality and increase participants' candor. Answers that emerge during the exercise (as described in bullet points below) are noted on flip chart paper. Typically, between ten and thirty-five people participate in the process. Participants should represent all levels and departments in the organization. Even though we were only assessing the culture of compliance at Islington-Barrett, we involved people from all aspects of the company, since compliance was a company-wide concern.

The goal of the process was to gain a deeper understanding of how the Islington-Barrett culture of compliance operated, and how underlying assumptions were both helping and hindering its cultural system. Here are the steps in the culture assessment process that we used:

> **Review the purpose, expectations, and goal for the day.** Islington-Barrett's purpose was to explore how current cultural assumptions were barriers to moving compliance from a chore to an opportunity and benefit.

> **Present a brief overview of culture.** Shared a definition of organizational culture. (Please reference Chapter 1 for a definition of organizational culture and related definitions).

> **Elicit descriptions of cultural artifacts.** Asked participants to list aspects of culture that can be observed or felt. (Artifacts are defined at the beginning of Step 3 in this chapter).

> **Identify espoused values.** Asked participants to list expressed values and beliefs. (Values are defined at the beginning of Step 3 in this chapter).

> **Identify shared underlying assumptions.** Guided participants through a process of identifying unconscious, taken for granted beliefs and values that drive perception, behavior, thought, and feeling in an organizational culture. We arrive at underlying assumptions by finding places where the *artifacts and values contradict each other*. For example, if you have a value such as "acting strategically" and people are constantly putting out daily fires (a behavioral artifact), then you have a

contradiction. As Edgar Schein says,[38] the key to identifying underlying assumptions is to check "whether the espoused values that have been identified really explain the all of the artifacts or whether things that have been described as going on have clearly *not* been explained or are in actual conflict with values articulated". He then goes to say, "Once assumptions are made conscious, this usually triggers a whole new set of insights and begins to make sense of a whole range of things that previously had not made sense."

» **Identify how your culture helps and hinders creating a more proactive, integrated approach to compliance.** Cultures almost always both help and hinder their progress toward reaching goals or making changes. If you're working with more than fifteen people, have your group split in half and discuss how the culture is helping and hindering the cultural changes they'd like to make. Islington-Barrett chose to continue working as one group during this discussion.

» **Decide on next steps.** Asked participants to make decisions on next steps.

Below are lists of what we uncovered after spending a half-day with Islington-Barrett. As you can see, the company generated lengthy lists. There's power in being able to see key artifacts, values, and assumptions all in one place. These lists give organizational members an opportunity to stand outside the day-to-day culture and look at it more holistically and objectively.

Islington-Barrett's artifacts, values, and cultural assumptions

Artifacts

» Operate as teams

» Lots of deadlines; some missed due dates

» Compliance is open to interpretation and has the potential for errors

» Calendar of meetings—represents a lack of time

» Communication can lag (right people getting the right message at the right time)

- » Hard to see the spokes and pieces and how they connect
- » Safe and transparent conversations when need to resolve a compliance issue
- » Competing priorities
- » Compliance is a moving target
- » Going above and beyond gets rewarded
- » Working to keep up with new compliance requirement
- » Reactive to compliance
- » Don't always reflect on past standards and actions
- » Relying on others to handle compliance
- » Positive stakeholder relationships
- » People willingly help when asked
- » Lack of consistency—need to improve (in part due to reactive nature)
- » Decision-making is contextually driven
- » Desire and commitment to be compliant
- » Successful compliance program
- » Hit or miss documentation

Values

- » Success
- » Trust
- » Respect
- » Be the best
- » To be challenged
- » Safety
- » Ease and streamlining
- » Do the right thing
- » Willing to help
- » Doing the hard work
- » Focus on the future
- » Innovation
- » Enjoying our jobs
- » Doing a great job: taking pride in work
- » Learning culture
- » People matter
- » High expectations
- » Teamwork
- » Empowerment
- » Agility
- » How things get done is just as important as the results
- » Expertise
- » Peer review
- » Varied opinions; inclusivity

Cultural assumptions

- » We don't say no
- » People are overextended
- » Compliance shouldn't take this much time
- » Compliance and daily work are not the same
- » Compliance is the compliance team's responsibility
- » More training will fix situation
- » Adding more resources will resolve situation
- » We do what needs to be done, even when it's not strategic or it's repetitive
- » Fear of failure (because we need "to be the best," "do the right thing," we're not taking risks to try something new)
- » Not all team members are recognized
- » Proving that we're compliant is a chore

In Chapter 5, we'll learn how Islington-Barrett resolved the underlying cultural assumptions that were holding them back and transformed them with the Adaptogen Design process. But how does this apply to your organization? Your lists of artifacts, behaviors, and underlying assumptions may look very different than Islington-Barrett's list. The goal is to uncover the underlying assumptions and beliefs driving mindset and behavior in your culture. That's when you'll hit pay dirt and can begin identifying how your culture is both helping and hindering your organization's move toward brilliance.

Chart your system

Ask each team or department to draw their cultural system and then compare notes. Use these questions to help you think about your system: How would you diagram the operation of your team or department's cultural system? How do people interact and communicate within your team or department? How would you describe the system at the level of mindset, behavior, and structure?

With what other systems does your cultural system interact? In what ways do they interact? What's the quality of the interaction (disengaged, sporadic, or conflictual, or positive and productive)?

Mindset, perception, and assumptions—how we perceive our experiences can dramatically impact how and what we learn, and what we learn impacts the evolution of our culture and our willingness to change.

We'll discuss this in more detail in Chapter 4. But I'll say this for now: People change when they understand why, when they have input, when they understand their role and how they can contribute, when they rally around something larger than themselves, when they can trust, when they have a voice, and when they are allowed to solve problems. People resist change when it requires them to grow and they aren't guided to do so, when the elephant isn't named, and when they are forced, betrayed, or feel that they have no recourse. That's why the Cultural Brilliance System is so inclusive. Because it just makes sense.

By the end of the Authenticity Phase, you have begun to witness and understand your cultural system more clearly. In the next chapter, the Contextual Emergence transition, we take what you've learned, validate it, and prepare to shape your brilliant culture.

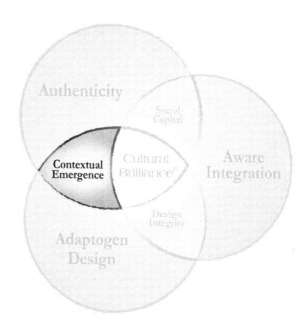

CHAPTER FOUR

CONTEXTUAL EMERGENCE TRANSITION

YOU'VE LOOKED YOUR ELEPHANT SQUARELY IN THE eyes. Now you have a deeper, more authentic understanding of how your cultural system operates. Congratulations. That kind of truth telling takes courage and you did it. Not only have you excavated old cultural beliefs and assumptions, you've paved the way for a new reality to emerge—the brilliance of your culture.

In this chapter, we shift gears and decide how you want to use what you've uncovered. We're in the transition between the Authenticity and Adaptogen Design Phases called Contextual Emergence. This transition is a brief stopping off point before we dive into designing your new cultural system in Chapter 5.

55

Contextual Emergence simply helps you to answer this question: Within the context of your organizational objectives, what's emerging that you'll want to weave into the new cultural system? In this chapter, we start to categorize your cultural discoveries into the three levels of mindset, behavior, and structure. Why? Because it's easiest to shift a cultural system by leveraging either mindset, behavior, or structure. In Chapter 5, in the Adaptogen Design Phase, we will explore these distinctions and leverage points more fully.

The goal of the Contextual Emergence transition is to determine the mindsets, behaviors, and structures that support your company's brilliance and the mindsets, behaviors, and structures that block your organizational growth—your brilliance and your blocks, for short. We'll discuss questions such as

1. Which of your cultural artifacts, values, and underlying assumptions do you want to bring forward into your new cultural design?

2. Which ones no longer serve you?

3. What's the emerging brilliance? In other words, how does what's best about you need to evolve?

4. How does this evolution support your company's purpose and business objectives?

Contextual Emergence also sets the stage for the future state of the culture by establishing a communication plan, right from the get-go, to preview steps in the cultural evolution process. People's buy-in, feedback, and insights are critical to the success of the transition, so they're intentionally integrated in this phase. This allows you to capture the energy and movement of transition, communicate with intention, and gather feedback so that the changes fully embody and reflect your people.

Lastly, the process of transition, the fundamental role of listening to self, others, and the cultural system, and that behavioral driver—mindset—are explored in this chapter. It's important that leaders and the teams that work with them understand how to harness the pivotal energy of transition. Understanding these pieces will help your company design a brilliant culture that decreases stress, inspires learning, and promotes organizational health.

In this chapter, we'll focus on three steps:

Step one: Harness the energies of transition, listening, and mindset

Step two: Identify your cultural system's brilliance and blocks

Step three: Develop a communication plan for optimal engagement

▸ **STEP ONE:**
Harness the energies of transition, listening, and mindset

The energy of transition

During the Authenticity Phase, the inner workings of your cultural system are illuminated and revealed in new and different ways. After that exploration, people's minds usually start to open to new possibilities, including the perspective that positive changes could be on the horizon. For many, it begins to seem possible that previously intractable problems are solvable, stress could diminish, and creativity, innovation, and growth could emerge. The potential of positive change is energizing—and we want to harness that energy.

Until this point, your cultural system has most likely reacted habitually to external stimuli, communication breakdowns, and problems. Now, we've started to create conditions in which mindset and behavioral patterns can be disrupted. After reacting habitually, the cultural system has the opportunity to shift into more intentional patterns and to learn every time it adapts. But meaningful learning required to navigate this transition comes with an emotional risk—the decision to move outside our cultural and individual comfort zones.

Let me explain by drawing on William Bridges' work here. Bridges was an organizational consultant and author of the groundbreaking book *Transitions: Making Sense of Life's Changes.*[39] His works made the crucial distinction between change and transition. Change is an event, such as getting a promotion, losing a job, or moving to a new city, but transition is the psychological process of adapting to the change event. As you can imagine, transition is the more challenging of the two processes, but it's also the richer one. Bridges says that it's in the "neutral zone" of transition that we can harness the energies of creativity, innovation, and growth.

The same is true with cultural transition—during Contextual Emergence, we begin to identify what's ending, where we are in transition, and what might be beginning. That's why it's so important to continuously *give people context* for the cultural evolution they've embarked upon, especially when it might be uncomfortable. It's helpful to remind your workforce of the fruit that discomfort will bear. Transition feels temporarily uncomfortable and can require an identity shift.

Years ago, I worked with facilities managers at a large institution. Although most had worked for many years at this institution, all were new to their management roles. Despite having been bestowed the title of manager, they had the identity of a tradesperson. In fact, the first time I met with them, they essentially said, "We're tradespeople. We are responsible for making sure this institution functions." We worked together to create a pathway for their identities to expand from being tradespeople to tradespeople and managers. Until their mindsets aligned with their new reality, role, and culture, they were stuck with old mindsets in a new environment—never a comfortable or healthy experience.

During the Contextual Emergence transition, SN Controls faced a similar experience. SN Controls discovered that an avoidance of direct, open conversations was a "block" holding the cultural system back from its ability to handle organizational growth and change. In a meeting with the entire company, we discussed the importance of moving through temporary discomfort to reach a healthier culture. As people began to communicate more directly, this new behavior was woven into the cultural system's fabric and did, in fact, evolve into a new norm. Once this norm was established, it was much more comfortable for all involved.

The energy of listening

The ability to harness the energy of transition is greatly enhanced by open-minded listening. In most cultures, there's a shortage of active listening. We listen for what we want to hear, what we hope to hear, and/or avoid what we don't want to hear. Part and parcel of looking the "elephant squarely in the eyes" is the willingness and courage to listen to what you hear. Remember that culture in and of itself is neutral and is a product of an organization's shared history. In other words, how we behave today is, in part, influenced by our historical culture.

As I work with organizations during the Contextual Emergence transition, I'll periodically say, "Let's stop and listen. What are we hearing? What's emerging in this conversation? What's beginning to change or shift?" During all phases of the Cultural Brilliance System, we want to help people to become more self-aware: to tune into what's going on inside themselves and within the cultural systems; to be aware of how their individual mindsets are creating a collective experience. Being culturally intelligent includes asking questions: What are people discussing? What's changing? What's stuck? Where are people's behaviors misaligned—in positive or negative ways—with the current culture?

Dr. Diana Whitney says that "Human systems grow in the direction of what they persistently ask questions about."[40] If you can listen to your teams, you can take what they value and build on it: *If you can listen to it, you can architect it.* The same principle applies to cultural systems—if you can listen to it, really hear the truth of it, the reality of it—you can architect something better. But first we need to understand the contextual landscape of the culture we inhabit.

The energy of mindset

As we discuss what's emerged from the Authenticity Phase, we notice, even more than ever, that mindsets are contagious. We know this when we discuss "bad apples" at work, mention that the same person always "poisons" team projects, or refer to the "brilliant jerk" in our engineering department. Mindsets drive and, and at times, unconsciously influence our behavior. Mindsets are driving the behavior of your culture right now.

As Carol Dweck notes,[41] people who believe their talent can be developed (especially in coordination with input from others, embracing solid strategies forward, and working hard) tend to achieve more. She refers to this state of mind as a growth mindset and notes that it allows higher achievement because people worry less about the perception of their efforts (as opposed to those with fixed mindsets who believe talents are innate, for instance) and instead put more of their energy into learning and further development. This is important both on an individual level and especially when it comes to overall company culture.

When entire companies embrace a growth mindset as part of their culture, team members note greater engagement with their work, as well as greater commitment to the organization and the organization's aims. Consider how this contrasts with what Dweck terms fixed-mindset companies where employees report far more cheating, deception, and lies in a zero-sum culture.

In brilliant cultures, these self-aware mindsets are critical because they springboard your company's ability to respond to change and recognize opportunities for learning. Ideally, we would check our mindsets daily and ask, "How is my mindset impacting my behavior, my outlook, and my interaction with other people?"

> » Dr. Pat Baccili, founder and CEO of Transformation Talk Radio, says that she doesn't solve problems. She instead immediately reframes any obstacle as an opportunity by asking, "What's possible in this situation?" Asking this question immediately moves our conscious and unconscious minds into possibilities beyond problem-solving, which stops us from regurgitating what's happened. It generates a thought process that moves us forward instead of holding us back.

> » Another favorite mindset check-in question is from Steve Chandler, author of a number of books, including *Crazy Good*, *Wealth Warrior*, and *Right Now*: "Given all that, what would you like to create?"[42] Given all of the circumstances, obstacles, or stories in your mind, what would you like to create in this situation? Like Dr. Pat's question, this one invites us to shift into a new realm of possibility instead of staying stuck in what we don't want. This is mindset work at its best. If you can change your mindset, you can change your behavior, and then you can change your outcome. The same is true for entire cultures.

> » Another good standard mindset check-in is "What have I/we learned?"

> » The question "What's the mindset in the room today?" almost always heightens self-awareness and causes people to tune into the interactions, group dynamics, and energy in the room.

Here's the thing: We are always in a mindset, so we might as well surface it. Naming our mindset automatically brings a higher level of consciousness, self-awareness, and systems awareness into the room. That's what mindset is all about: Do we understand how our beliefs, perceptions, and interpretations are enhancing or getting in the way of our behavior?

▶ **STEP TWO:**
Identify your cultural system's brilliance and blocks

Our steps here are practical ones as we continue to "look the elephant squarely in the eyes" by creating a Cultural Profile. Once you conclude the Authenticity Phase, you've generated a lot of information about your cultural systems and should be armed with both new and affirmed knowledge.

Remember the Cultural Safety Zone? This is a good time to check in and reengage this safe space. Although trust and psychological safety are not required to begin the Authenticity Phase, we ideally start building more trust as the cultural "truths" are revealed. In other words, we need to examine objectively, and without judgment, what we've learned in the Authenticity Phase. We also need to honor, respect, and value what has emerged.

When I create a Cultural Profile, I like to divide what the organization has learned into two categories: brilliance (What helps your company succeed?) and blocks (What holds your company back?) with three levels in each category: mindset, behavior, and structure. Where does information come from? During the Authenticity Phase, you should have gathered information through Discovery Interviews, the CultureTalk Survey, the Culture Assessment Process, Charting your System, or similar assessments and exercises. That's the information you're going to organize into brilliance and blocks columns.

As you review the insights, information, and underlying assumptions you've collected, you'll also want to distill them into mindsets (*beliefs, values, mental models, and emotions*), behavior (*interaction, communication, decision-making, and execution*), and structure (*environment, processes, and organizational design*).

Brilliance and Blocks

	BRILLIANCE	BLOCKS
Mindset:		
Behavior:		
Structure:		

Important note: Once you've organized your information in a Brilliance and Blocks Chart, you'll present this information to your entire company or representatives of all levels and areas of the company (depending on the organizational size) for 1.) Confirmation of accuracy, and 2.) Discussion of the interaction between mindsets, behaviors, and structures.

Below you'll find SN Controls' Cultural Profile, using a Brilliance and Blocks Chart.

SN Controls' Cultural Profile

Mindset (Underlying beliefs)	
Brilliance: What Helps SN Controls Succeed?	**Blocks: What Holds SN Controls Back?**
We care about meeting customer needs.	Preserving a relationship is often prioritized over what's best for the overall team.
We care about each other.	It's easier to do things myself rather than have a direct, honest conversation.
Socially responsible and environmentally conscious.	We don't raise issues or ask questions because we don't want to ruffle feathers.
Everyone can fit into our culture—we value longevity.	We don't ask "why" enough.

Mindset (Underlying beliefs)	
Brilliance: What Helps SN Controls Succeed?	**Blocks: What Holds SN Controls Back?**
It's more important to get product out the door.	We don't want to take responsibility for decisions (because we don't want to be blamed).
We wear multiple hats (should be able to do this, but shouldn't need to).	It's more important to get product out the door.
Customer needs come before internal needs.	We think like a small company.
We drop everything to get the job done.	We don't have time.
We think like a small (family) company.	We drop everything to get the job done.
	We've always done it this way.
	We hope someone else will fix a problem.
	We wear multiple hats (too busy to train people, tasks don't get delegated).
	We're too busy to plan or communicate long-term goals when we take on new products. This results in stress, negativity, and lack of buy-in.
	It's demoralizing and stressful when we don't meet deadlines for coworkers or customers.

Behavior	
Brilliance: What Helps SN Controls Succeed?	**Blocks: What Holds SN Controls Back?**
Work hard to get the job done; be determined.	Don't speak up often enough.
Act heroically to meet customer needs.	Blaming and finger pointing.
Be flexible, responsive, and trustworthy with customers.	Lack of long-term problem-solving and planning.
People are friendly and willing to help each other.	People and process problems are worked around, at times, instead of addressing and resolving the problems directly.
Longevity: People stay at the company.	Training/cross-training takes a back seat to getting the product out.
Good sense of humor.	No plan B (the assumption is that great ideas will work).
Welcoming to new people.	New people aren't fully trained, so can't relieve workload.
Lots of tribal knowledge (a positive as long as it gets documented).	Firefighting is relied on to solve problems rather than root cause analysis, strategy, and planning.
Work in a unique niche/have a unique manufacturing process.	Lack of positive feedback.
	Experience high stress.
	Don't always listen to what you hear.

Behavior	
Brilliance: What Helps SN Controls Succeed?	**Blocks: What Holds SN Controls Back?**
	Meetings range from productive to inefficient.
	Need to document tribal knowledge.
	Schedule/ship changes often aren't communicated to all who need that information.
	Don't revisit/relocate space usage once a product is in regular production.

Structure/System	
Brilliance: What Helps SN Controls Succeed?	**Blocks: What Holds SN Controls Back?**
Positive energy in facility.	The right information isn't getting to the right people at the right time.
A clean, open facility.	Work processes and instructions need more clarity.
Highly compliant with federal regulations.	Processes no longer needed (but still used) or over-refined cause extra work.
Potential customers who tour become customers.	Hiring/retention issues (health insurance cost may impact this).

Structure/System	
Brilliance: What Helps SN Controls Succeed?	**Blocks: What Holds SN Controls Back?**
Company is growing quickly.	QC turnaround time.
Work centers have good flow.	Disorganized areas; wasted physical space.
	Equipment not always fixed on time.
	Temperatures aren't always comfortable.

Confirmation of accuracy

After SN Controls reviewed its Cultural Profile, we organized a meeting to discuss questions like these:

> » What are the themes and trends emerging from the cultural information?
>
> » What's the emerging brilliance? The core of your cultural brilliance usually lies in using your cultural strengths intentionally and not overusing them to the point of creating a blind spot. A question that points to brilliance is "What's best about us that needs to evolve? How?"
>
> » Which blocks—at the levels of mindset, behavior, and structure—are most important to address?
>
> » Which areas of brilliance—at the levels of mindset, behavior, and structure—are most important to keep?

Based on the information, perspectives, and ideas gathered, we then discussed these key questions: Based on this information, what culture do we need to create/foster/grow to proactively adapt to change in ways that decrease stress, inspire learning, and promote organizational health? Are we still solving the same cultural problem? Or do these areas of brilliance or blocks indicate there's a different or deeper cultural issue to address?

How does our brilliance align with our purpose and business objectives? How do our blocks stop us from achieving our organizational goals and living our organizational purpose? Most of the time, the brilliance and the blocks align with the original concern, but it's always best to confirm that this is true and accurate.

Discussion of the interaction between mindsets, behaviors, and structures

After we've confirmed that the cultural system's brilliance and blocks align with the cultural problem the organization needs to solve, we move on to the second phase of discussing the Cultural Profile—analyzing how the mindsets, behaviors, and structures interact with other. It's not uncommon for a mindset to be the catalyst for behavior or the structure in a system. I've also worked with cultural systems in which a certain set of behaviors set the stage for mindset, or an organizational structure contextualizes both mindset and behavior in positive or negative ways.

Examples include

» In some companies, conflict gets avoided, a common behavioral response. When conflict is avoided often enough, mindsets develop about conflict that are usually counterproductive, such as "conflict is negative," "we work around others when conflict develops," or "it's someone else's fault." These mindsets and avoidant behavior usually wreak havoc on systems and processes throughout the organization. Here's why: If we can't resolve differences, how can we solve problems or make decisions when a system or process breaks down?

» We've all been in meetings in which people listen silently and participation is rare. In addition to being boring, those meetings usually indicate that attendees don't feel emotionally safe or comfortable to voice thoughts, opinions, or new ideas. They also may not feel valued. There's almost always an underlying mindset (cultural belief) driving the behavior. An extreme example of this dynamic was the Challenger example in Chapter 3, in which managers didn't listen to engineers. Over time, engineers stopped speaking up.

As SN Controls discussed the interaction between their mindsets, behaviors, and structures, they noticed that the mindset of "prioritizing a relationship over what's best for the entire team" and these related mindsets—

> » It's easier to do things myself rather than have a direct, honest conversation.
>
> » We don't raise issues or ask questions because we don't want to ruffle feathers.
>
> » We don't ask "why" enough.
>
> » We don't want to take responsibility for decisions (because we don't want to be blamed).

—caused the "work-arounds" in the Behavioral Blocks section. Fear of hurting others' feelings, stepping on people's toes, or having a difficult conversation resulted in many people working around someone they didn't want to work with, deal with, or confront. These "work-arounds" drained productivity, emotional energy, and stopped important company-wide conversations from happening. The SN Controls workforce developed a behavioral habit of tolerating people and problems instead of arranging for a direct, honest conversation to resolve the issue.

▸ STEP THREE:
Develop a communication plan for optimal engagement

The goal of the communication plan is two-fold: to keep people informed and engaged, and to continue to create an intentional space to design the new version of the cultural system. In most organizations, I again nod to the insightful contribution of William Bridges and use his 4 Ps process for communicating change: Purpose, Picture, Plan, and Part.[43] Let's look at how each P applies to the Cultural Brilliance System.

> » **Purpose:** Why are we designing a new culture? What problem are we solving? What are we trying to accomplish? Human beings need to understand the logic of a change before they can change, and this is especially true for a cultural transition.
>
> » **Picture:** What is the end game? How is it going to work? What is evolving and what isn't? People often need to

imagine what the new cultural system will look like before they can give their hearts to it.

» **Plan:** What is the road map for getting to where we need to go? What is going to happen over the next several months? What happens first, second, third? People need a clear idea of how they are going to get to where they need to go.

» **Part:** What is my role? How will I be involved? Do I have an opportunity for input on the plan? When will I be trained? What's the optimal mindset and/or behavior for me to adopt during the process? People need a tangible way to contribute.

You'll want to develop a clear communication plan and distribute it to your entire organization, tailoring it to specific departments or teams as needed. You'll also want to be sure to update it at regular intervals as you move through the Cultural Brilliance System and make sure that you have a designated "owner" of this critical task.

During Contextual Emergence, we start acting on the cultural truth that's been revealed. There are three steps in receiving the truth:

» *Be willing to listen to the truth.*

» *Be willing to acknowledge its validity.*

» *Be willing to act on what's learned and validated.*

Number three—act on what you've learned—is essential in the Cultural Brilliance System and, indeed, in any organizational change. Years ago, I led one arm of a consulting project for a state agency. The project was important and the people were committed, but no one would act on several issues that were raised. For example, there was a high level of disorganization that impacted project outcomes. When I pointed out this behavioral pattern, the response was "You're right. We own that behavior, and we are responsible for it"—but they did nothing to rectify the situation. Instead, the cultural system spent time in high drama. People ran around being extremely busy but took very little action to resolve or improve chronic situations that everyone disliked, and that impeded organizational effectiveness. They had a cultural assumption that they "were doing the best they could" while it was obvious to anyone outside the system that they could easily remedy several long-standing issues. But part of their cultural identity included being long-suffering, committed public servants who never had enough resources. So even when straightforward solutions presented themselves, they were not able to act on them. Unaware of the cultural assumption and cultural identity, they were, in fact, caught in a blind spot that prevented them from evolving into a new level of organization effectiveness.

During the Culture Profile process, I remind participants that they are in the transition of emerging into a new cultural system, and thus, can't yet know what size and shape the butterfly will be as it emerges after its metamorphosis. Together we remember to listen, notice the energy, and be aware of our mindsets. We are setting the stage for new mindsets, behaviors, and structures to emerge. During the next chapter, Adaptogen Design, we create a road map for bringing what has been learned, revealed, and embraced to life in your organization.

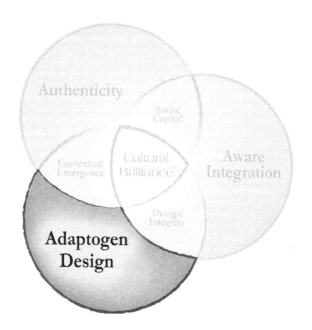

CHAPTER FIVE

ADAPTOGEN DESIGN PHASE: THE VISION OF CULTURE

AS WE ENTER PHASE TWO OF THE CULTURAL Brilliance System, Adaptogen Design, we've learned a tremendous amount about the inner working of your workplace culture, including the places it shines and the places it could use polish. During the Adaptogen Design Phase, you'll learn how to move your cultural system from its current state to its new, brilliant form. To accomplish this task, we'll build on what we've learned through the Authenticity Phase and the Contextual Emergence transition.

Why is this phase of the Cultural Brilliance System called Adaptogen Design? An adaptogen is a natural substance, such as an herbal medicine like ginseng or maca, considered to help the body adapt to stress and to exert a normalizing effect upon bodily processes.[44] The origin of "adaptogen" is the word *adapto* meaning "to adapt" and the suffix *gen* meaning "producing." As a result, an adaptogen is a system or entity that adapts and produces.

Let's look at what adaptogen means in the human body to understand how the term relates to the Cultural Brilliance System. For example, ginseng is well-known for its adaptogenic properties such as supporting physical endurance, mental clarity, and antioxidant properties supportive of both heart health and a healthy immune system. Like other adaptogens, it helps to both stabilize physiological processes and promote homeostasis—or a sense of balance within the body.

When we look at the adaptogenic properties of brilliant cultures, you can readily see this at play: Brilliant cultures stabilize the health of the system because they proactively respond to change in ways that decrease stress, inspire learning, and promote organizational growth—**so they are inherently adaptogen in nature.** Cultures evolve into brilliance as they start to understand, adapt to, and embrace change, not as something to be resisted, but as something to be experienced differently. Instead of viewing change as a force to resist, change becomes perceived as a part of the natural rhythm of organizational life. An Adaptogen Design™ allows an organization to build up stores of strength, creativity, and resilience as it learns from each iterative adaptation to change.

This chapter provides a practical course in how to activate an adaptogen design—including strategies, tools, and best practices. Systems, energy, and resistance all play an important role in this design process, toward which Design Teams, mindset paradigms, and feedback methods can all be effective tools. Principles of design thinking and systems thinking form the backbone of the design process. Through the Adaptogen Design Phase, questions are asked, like "What's the underlying logic in the design?" "Is the design coherent and aligned with organizational systems?" "Does it meet the needs of people, communication, and energy?"

A design may work on paper, but Adaptogen Design requires a knowledge and respect for the cultural systems at play, the fact that human beings respond to energetic inputs, and that when people resist, there may be a good reason. As a result, in this chapter we look at principles of organizational transition, including giving people a forum to voice concerns, a leading hand in the cultural design process, and discussing points of tension as they arise. The goal is to get people in the right conversation so that behavioral reality matches the cultural design.

As Govindarajan and Trimble[45] note, "Gaps are sustained by a 'dominant logic' or mindset that is entrenched in the culture." Adaptogen Design addresses those gaps by charting a course for cultural evolution so that organizations adapt to rapid change in ways that increase sustainability, engagement, and innovation.

In this chapter, we'll focus on these three steps:

Step one: Understand your individual role in change

Step two: Learn the three-step Adaptogen Design process

Step three: Decide how to apply and execute the design process

▶ STEP ONE:
Understand your individual role in change

Understanding your role during change involves understanding how identity and systems interact. We know that systems in nature change in seemingly perfect coherence. The seasons move from one to another, waves respond to gravitational pull, and one species keeps another in check through predation. The one big difference is that nature and animals don't have the same sense of identity that humans do. And that's where we get into trouble. Often, we attach our identity to our physical state, careers, or expertise. When something changes outside of ourselves, we sometimes resist it because, at a fundamental level, our identity is challenged. When we remember that cultural systems are mindsets, behaviors, and structures that sequence in patterns that drive organizational decision-making, communication, and results, the role of identity, which impacts mindset and behavior, is especially important.

When you sense resistance within, ask yourself: Am I resisting this change because it scares me or makes me uncomfortable? Or because I believe it is not in the culture's best interest? And finally, if I think it's not in the culture's best interest, am I telling myself that because I'm afraid or uncomfortable? If this sounds circular, that's because it is. Why do people feel fear or discomfort? Because we are asking them to grow, and by asking them to grow, we are asking them to alter—before, during, or after a change—an aspect of themselves and their sense of who they are.

Here's the rub. As humans, we are meant to grow and evolve both cognitively and emotionally. Adults who get stuck in their development or don't have the opportunity to grow at work are typically dissatisfied. As Kegan and Lahey describe in *An Everyone Culture: Becoming a Deliberately Developmental Organization,* "As human beings we're set up to protect ourselves—but it is just as true that we're set up to grow psychologically, to evolve, to develop. In fact, research shows that the single biggest cause of work burnout is not work overload, but working too long without experiencing your own personal development."[46]

During Adaptogen Design, we shift perspectives by looking at change as a necessary, natural state to be embraced rather than feared or resisted. How do we shift that paradigm? By understanding that when we eschew change, what we are often avoiding is how a change makes us feel, not whether it's beneficial. When we don't understand the context for what's happening inside us and/or outside us during change, we do what any normal person would do: We put on the proverbial brakes to give ourselves time to determine what's going on or to become comfortable again. During Adaptogen Design, we involve people from all parts of the organization in the design process, provide context, and, ultimately, make changes in the culture that are intentional. If people are uncomfortable, they are encouraged to check in with themselves to determine if the discomfort is a "gut feeling" that something is wrong or if they are moving outside their comfort zone.

By listening to themselves and each other, people use their cultural intelligence to notice signals from the cultural system. These signals can take the form of conflict, mental or emotional stuckness, or repetitive mistakes, for example. Conflict can be a sign that a relationship or process wants to change. What used to work, no longer works. Teams get mentally or emotionally stuck when they are mired in organizational politics, when they don't feel safe to tell the truth, or when they refuse to grow along with the culture. Repetitive mistakes often stem from disengagement or a faulty system or process. In any of these cases, we look to the cultural system. Most people want to resolve problems and be engaged. If they aren't, they may be drinking a cultural Kool-Aid of disengagement or feeling frustrated.

During Authenticity we've already uncovered many of these cultural signals and during Adaptogen Design, we'll decide how to restore them to balance and health.

▶ STEP TWO:
Learn the three-step Adaptogen Design process

Now we move into the nuts and bolts of Adaptogen Design process itself. Here in step two, we'll learn the three-step Adaptogen Design process, and how to work with the key leverage points of mindset, behavior, and structure. Then, in step three, we'll focus on tools, strategies, and teams you can use to put the Adaptogen process into action.

Adaptogen Design relies on the principles of both systems thinking and design thinking, which we'll explore later in the section. But what do we mean by design? Buckminster Fuller describes design as "the process by which intentions are realized."[47] When we use the word *design*, we are describing how we will turn an idea or vision into reality. In other words, design is simply our path forward that bridges our current culture and our brilliant culture. This path forward will functionally outline how we will move our cultural system from where it is now to where we want it to be.

The work you've done on understanding your organization's cultural systems further allows you to design at three levels—mindset, behavior, and structure. Recognizing the need for all three levels to be fully involved will allow your culture to evolve in a state of awareness. As participants in the Adaptogen Design process individuals in your culture will need to reconsider their mindset, be open to learning, and step into the discomfort and excitement of growth.

In a nutshell, Adaptogen Design™ is a three-step process:

> » **Contextual Emergence:** What mindsets, behaviors, and structures do you want to bring forward? And what do you want to leave behind?
>
> » **Systems:** How does the cultural system operate? What are cultural subsystems and how do they interact with each other? What are the leverage points in the system?
>
> » **Design:** What solution (or leverage point) will move the cultural system from its current state into a brilliant state?

Now let's look at each step in more detail.

Contextual Emergence

What mindsets, behaviors, and structures do you want to bring forward? And what do you want to leave behind?

During the Contextual Emergence transition in Chapter 4, we identified the mindsets, behaviors, and structures your organization wants to keep and release, and the new ones it wants to adopt. This is where we begin to use them, during the first step of the Adaptogen Design process. To get started,

> » You'll want to conduct a brief review to ensure your organization is up to speed on the outcomes of the Contextual Emergence transition.
>
> » You'll want to revisit the cultural problem you're trying to solve, and particularly the blocks you want to resolve during the Adaptogen Design Phase.
>
> » You'll also want to reiterate the goal of the design process: to decide how your cultural system will move from its current state into its brilliant state, in whatever form you've identified that needs to take.

Remember Islington-Barrett, the company from Chapter 3? By the time it was ready to design its culture of compliance, it discovered three big gaps. Although the Director recognized that compliance was considered an extra chore, she and the company had not fully internalized the extent to which compliance wasn't integrated into daily work. This mindset was revealed during the Authenticity Phase when an engineer said, "I don't even consider compliance standards when I create a technical design." The second gap was the mindset that "We do what needs to be done, even if it's not strategic or it's repetitive." The third mindset was a common one: "If we devote more resources to compliance, it will become less stressful." Sometimes, more resources—hiring more people or increasing a budget—are needed. Stay tuned, though, to find out what happens here. Islington-Barrett set out to design a culture of compliance that incorporated compliance into everyday work and solved problems with innovation. Both stemmed from having a strategic and proactive mindset.

Systems

How does the cultural system operate? What are cultural subsystems and how do they interact with each other? What are the leverage points in the system?

In Chapter 2, we defined a system as a group of consistently interacting people, concepts, or physical objects that form a unified whole. All systems are influenced by their environment and are part of other larger systems. In *Thinking in Systems: A Primer*, Donella Meadows says that the things making up the system "are interconnected in such a way that they produce their own pattern of behavior over time. The system may be buffeted, constricted, triggered, or driven by outside forces. But the system's response is characteristic of itself, and that response is seldom simple in the real world."[48]

Meadows makes an incredibly critical point we want to keep in mind: Systems produce their own pattern of behavior over time. As a result, no two cultural systems are alike. It's the behavior of the system and the people in it that give us a window into how the system operates. This aligns with our definition that cultural systems are mindsets, behaviors, and structures that sequence in often unseen patterns that drive organizational decision-making, communication, and results.

In this second step of the Adaptogen Design process, we view what was learned in the Contextual Emergence transition through the lens of systems. When we look at the behavior of a cultural system, we usually see systems nested within systems or connected to larger systems, known as subsystems. Throughout the design process, we must consider and understand how these systems work in relationship to each other. For example, how does the communication system interact with the customer service system? In another example common to many companies, do the engineering system and the sales system work together, or do they clash? If we're redesigning the cultural system of a sales team, we can't do that in isolation because the sales function interacts with many other systems within a company and systems external to the company, such as customers and competitors. We need to understand how those systems behave in relationship to each other.

Let's examine Islington-Barrett's subsystems. As a reminder, the company's goal was to shift the culture of compliance from a burden to a benefit. During the Authenticity Phase and Contextual Emergence transition, we got to the root of what was blocking the cultural system from evolving.

For our purposes, Islington-Barrett's systems included the compliance team, executive team, engineering and IT teams, and organizational communication. Let's examine how each system functioned and interacted with one another.

Compliance team: As a system, it was burdened. The Director of Compliance and her team of three dedicated professionals were working overtime to keep the company compliant, and, in fact, they had passed an external audit with flying colors. But that was done on the backs of this team of four. The system was highly functional, but only due to the expertise and dedication of the four on the team, and the innovative problem-solving of the Director. When the team interacted with other systems in the company, it met resistance and complaints. No one liked having to deal with compliance, even though they understood that compliance created a rigorously safe environment for their workers and customers.

Executive team: As a system, this team maintained a more traditional hierarchical distance from the rest of the company. Even though this team sat in an open-space environment with the rest of the company, cared about the culture, and encouraged people to be innovative, in practice they could be gatekeepers to change. This system behaved cautiously and required a lot of input when changes were proposed.

Engineering and IT: These systems were also overburdened, overworked, and incredibly dedicated to the company. Although they still produced satisfactory results, they were only solving short-term problems due to their overloaded state. These departments talked about "not having time" to solve long-term problems and instead focused on "putting out fires." Although they wanted compliance to become less of a burden, they believed it wasn't their responsibility to resolve the situation.

Organizational communication: The communication system was effective in the sense that there were consistent, formal vehicles in place: CEO town halls, regular strategic off-sites, and other committees meeting to improve the organization. There was an internal website for organizational communication. Informal communication between departmental systems was less effective, partly because people were overworked and inundated with email and meeting requests. A high volume of meetings and emails have been shown to decrease productivity.[49]

At this point, it's a good idea to list all the subsystems you see in your cultural system. Then begin sketching out on paper how they operate, overlap, and interact:

> » How would you describe each subsystem? What works well? What are points of tension? When is it successful? When does it tend to fail or make significant mistakes? Where does it bottleneck? Remember, we are talking about the system, not specific people in the system.

> » How do these subsystems interact with each other? What does this interaction tell you about the cultural system?

SN Controls' list of systems included

> » Production
> » Communication
> » Training
> » Sales
> » Marketing
> » Compliance
> » Shipping and Receiving

> » Finance
> » Purchasing
> » Customers
> » Subcontractors
> » Quality Control
> » Humans Resources
> » Manufacturing

SN Controls' system

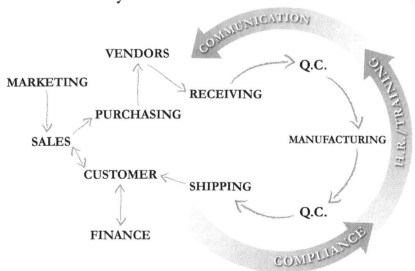

Donella Meadows says that systems have goals and rules and they create their own behavior based on how they are structured. The key to changing how a system behaves is to find leverage points—places in the system where a small change could lead to a large shift in cultural systems behavior[50]. In the Cultural Brilliance System, the key leverage or intervention points are generally mindset, behavior, and structure.

First, let's understand how leverage points work, and then we'll go back to Islington-Barrett and SN Controls to learn about their leverage points and how they used them to their advantage. Leverage points are the intervention points in systems; they are the fulcrum upon which change rests. For example, Martin Luther King Jr. and the campaign of nonviolent protests like sit-ins were so powerful because they highlighted the scope of the issue. In simple economic terms, the handful of restaurants that suffered because of the sit-ins should not have been such an easy target for huge change—and yet they were because they were highly visible places, and thus, a perfect leverage point.

Leverage points can be counterintuitive, though, as highlighted in the example of Martin Luther King and restaurant sit-ins. Often the counterintuitive nature of leverage points will cause organizations to push their system in the wrong direction.

The Club of Rome provides a great example of this. As Meadows explains, years ago the Club of Rome asked MIT systems analysis guru Jay Forrester to show how major global problems—such as unemployment, environmental destruction and resource depletion, poverty and hunger—might be related and, thus, solved. Forrester's computer model came out with a clear leverage point: growth. And in particular, the leverage point was not limited to population growth, but included economic growth even more so.

Now, at first glance this may not be surprising at all. After all, world leaders have been fixated on economic growth as an answer to nearly every problem for decades. Unfortunately, they're all too often pushing in the wrong direction. As Forrester's model noted, growth has costs, including ones we all too often ignore or push aside: poverty, hunger, resource depletion, environmental destruction. That is, what is actually needed is a much different kind of growth, a much slower and more sustainable growth, or no growth at all.

Meadows, as a result, identifies twelve leverage points or places to intervene in a system. For the sake of simplicity, we'll only review her top six leverage points[51] (in reverse order) **and then discuss how each one relates to the *Cultural Brilliance* leverage points of mindset, behavior, and structure.**

6. The structure of information flows (who does and does not have access to information). Who has access to information makes a tremendous difference in the power of that information. For instance, Meadows points to regulations in the mid '80s requiring factories to report their hazardous contaminant release numbers at the end of each year. Suddenly that information was available, and without any further increases in other regulations, by 1990, air pollutants dropped by more than 40 percent. Simply making that information more widely available was enough, as communities could put pressure on companies that were big polluters to do better. Similarly, who has access to information in our organizations makes a big difference in the power of that information. Information flow is its own power, and companies who rely strictly on hierarchy in information systems tend to suffer as a result. As Meadows notes, "Missing feedback is one of the most common causes of system malfunction."[52] In the Cultural Brilliance System, this leverage point often aligns with structure. One way Islington-Barrett shifted the culture of compliance from burden to benefit was to create a new structure that changed the flow of information, ideas, and problem-solving. We'll explore this experience in more depth later in the chapter.

5. The rules of the system (such as incentives, punishments, and constraints). All you need to do to realize the power of rules is to imagine your current system with different rules. If, for instance, your interns made corporate policy rather than your executive team, how differently would your company run? And the same is true for any system in which our organization works. Rules—such as incentives, punishments, and constraints—formalize who has power in a system. Who do your rules empower, and who do they disenfranchise? Answering those questions can often provide real insight into where you may have real cultural problems within your organization, as well as help account for voices that should be at the table but aren't. SN Controls shifted the rules of its systems when it moved from a more hierarchical structure to a system that emphasized individual ownership and empowerment. In its case, the leverage point was behavior. In Chapter 7, we'll unpack its process more fully.

4. The power to add, change, evolve, or self-organize the system structure. The ability to self-organize, to change, adapt, and evolve is fundamental to human survival, or, for that matter, the survival of any species. There's a reason that biologists worship genetic diversity and what it makes possible in evolution. And the same is true in an organizational sense. Ask yourself: How is your organization equipped for change and able to adapt? The less able it is to adapt, change, and respond, the less fluid your organizational culture is, and the less prospects you have for a long-term future. As Meadows puts it, "Insistence on a single culture shuts down learning. Cuts back resilience. Any system, biological, economic, or social, that gets so encrusted that it cannot self-evolve, a system that systematically scorns experimentation and wipes out the raw material of innovation, is doomed over the long term on this highly variable planet."[53] When I first began working with SN Controls, its culture had shut down learning and resisted change. As a result, the cultural system was not able to evolve when the company's sales volume increased. This inability to adapt led to temporarily serious consequences as stress levels skyrocketed and productivity plummeted. Fortunately, we were able to reverse these trends as we worked through the Cultural Brilliance System and unpacked the mindsets and behaviors keeping its cultural systems stuck.

3. The goals of the system. Of course, none of the above points matter if the goals of the system are not sustainable or healthy. For most corporations, the bottom-line goal is continual growth. Of course, that's also the goal of cancer, and if growth is always the goal, that will take precedence over other necessary parts of a healthy culture, such as self-organization, rules, a willingness to listen, or a willingness to step away from tradition when innovation is called for. As a result, it's incredibly important that we address the goals of our organization very clearly and closely. Yes, we want our business to grow. But ultimately, what is the end goal? Is it never-ending growth? That isn't healthy for communities, businesses, or the world; all empires eventually collapse on themselves in part because growth is not a sustainable goal unto itself. So be very clear about what the goal of your organization is, as that will affect every other piece of your culture. Mindset, behavior, and structure are all driven by the goals of the systems. Because brilliant cultures are adaptogen in nature, they seek sustainable, healthy goals. If the goals of your system are not healthy, your organization will not reach its potential brilliance. If this raises a question for you, please be sure to pause and reassess your goals.

2. Paradigms: The mindset out of which the system—its goals, structures, rules, delays, parameters—arises. Paradigms are mindsets that are socially accepted as true and, as such, are the hardest leverage point to activate. But we also know that paradigms can change. Once a large percentage of Americans believed it was well and good to own people, and while we believe skyscrapers are valuable real estate because they are at the center of the city, the sprawl of our suburbs is testament to the number of people who don't want to live downtown, much less raise a family there. To change paradigms, follow Thomas Kuhn's advice:[54] Keep pointing at the failures of the old paradigm and insert people from the new paradigm in places of visibility and power so they can be effective change agents. Focus on the middle ground of open-minded people, and change will come. SN Controls' cultural system was based on the paradigm that people waited for those above them in the hierarchy to direct them. When the company's sales volume increased and people needed to act more autonomously to solve problems as they arose, they couldn't. They were trapped in the old paradigm. As you'll see later in this and subsequent chapters, SN Controls worked diligently and successfully to shift its paradigm.

1. Transcending paradigms. Few people get here. The few that do, however, find it remarkably empowering. If you realize that any paradigm can be changed, then you realize that no rule is absolute, and there are truly no limits to what may be possible. It is to fully open the doors of possibility. Few people, and fewer organizations, can ever get there, but if they can, the sky truly is the limit. The Cultural Brilliance System offers companies the opportunity to transcend the paradigms that hold them back from their inherent brilliance, from their ability to make their greatest contributions to the world.

We won't hone in on specific leverage points for your cultural system until we begin our design work in step three of the Adaptogen Design process. Building on Meadows' emphasis that leverage points can be counterintuitive, *make sure to always explore the opposite of your leverage point*. Ask yourself: What if we pushed this leverage point in the opposite direction? If we think the leverage point is mindset, what would happen if we used structure? If we think it's structure, what would happen if we leveraged behavior?

Islington-Barrett recognized that people's mindsets toward compliance were a complicating factor. Even a mention of compliance was met with a lack of enthusiasm and quite possibly a groan. That de-energized mindset made it nearly impossible for people to think differently. Clearly, the mindset needed to shift into one with more positivity, possibility, and proactivity. Behavior toward compliance didn't allow for creative problem-solving and strategic planning. The Director of Compliance was often chasing people when they missed key compliance deadlines. Meeting to review new compliance standards was met with a lackluster response. Even though everyone agreed that the culture of compliance needed to change, they weren't convinced they were part of the problem or the solution (this is not uncommon). Finally, structure was a factor. As discussed earlier, the compliance team bore the weight of compliance for the entire company. This structure allowed others to self-select out of participating in creating a strategic, proactive compliance culture.

Let's go back to your answers to the cultural subsystems questions (from earlier in this Systems section). What potential leverage points can you identify?

Design

What solution (or leverage point) will move the cultural system from its current state to a brilliant state?

Now that you've explored the first two steps of the Adaptogen Design process, Contextual Emergence and Systems, it's time to move on to the third step, Design. During this step, we'll design the new mindsets, behaviors, and structures your organization needs to develop and integrate to create a brilliant culture. Then, in the next section of this chapter, we'll take a tour of the Design Teams, tools, and strategies you can use as vehicles to create your Adaptogen Design.

But first, let's take a quick tutorial on design thinking. Design thinking is a creative problem-solving process that incorporates an empathetic approach to meet the needs of people. It's an integrated "third way" that operates in the space between intuition/emotion and rational/analytical problem-solving. Design thinking is both strategic and empathetic because it combines what people want (desirability) with business needs (viability) and technological capability (feasibility).

The current CEO of IDEO, Tim Brown, describes design thinking as "a human-centered approach to innovation that draws from the designer's toolkit to integrate the needs of people, the possibilities of technology, and the requirements for business success."[55]

In addition to a design process, design thinking is a creative, solution-oriented mindset in alignment with the *Cultural Brilliance* goal of proactively responding to change in ways that decrease stress, inspire learning, and promote organizational health. When we design a brilliant culture, we want to keep Albert Einstein's words front and center: "We can't solve problems with the same thinking we used when we created them." This perspective is the heart and soul of Adaptogen Design.

Adaptogen Design principles

These are design principles to keep front and center as you plan your design process:

> » Systems stay resilient when they can evolve; try to control a system too tightly and you will most certainly extinguish its brilliance. Make sure your cultural systems—and the people in them—have room to breathe.
>
> » In most situations, people close to the problem solve the problem. At the same time, including people who are removed from a cultural issue is useful. They may be able to share new insights and are less likely to succumb to cultural blind spots.
>
> » You want to create a design that will allow your cultural system to rebalance itself when it loses direction, is hit with unexpected external stressors (like a new competitor breathing down your neck), or when even a planned internal shift causes undue stress.
>
> » Look for logic in the design. Is it coherent? Can you get from point A to point B easily? Is it clear how the design will create the desired result? If you need a ten-page manual to understand the design, it's time to head back to the drawing board. The most impactful designs are often the simplest; they hone in on a seemingly small leverage point that shifts the system in the right direction.
>
> » As Occam's razor states, "The simplest solution is usually the best one and the correct one."[56] Based on many years of experience working in organizations, I've added a corollary: "Complexity is not a sign of intelligence."

▶ STEP THREE:
Decide how to apply and execute the design process

Now we move on the practical application of the Adaptogen Design process. Here are the three steps again:

> » **Contextual Emergence:** What mindsets, behaviors, and structures do you want to bring forward? And what do you want to leave behind?
>
> » **Systems:** How does the cultural system operate? What are cultural subsystems and how do they interact with each other? What are the leverage points in the system?
>
> » **Design:** What solution (or leverage point) will move the cultural system from its current state to a brilliant state?

During the first step, Contextual Emergence, we analyzed your cultural system from the perspective of mindset, behavior, and structure. Then in second step, Systems, we examined how your cultural subsystems interact and we learned about leverage points. Now in the third step, we're answering the question, "What solution or leverage point will move the cultural system from its current state to a brilliant state?" To successfully execute all three steps, we need a vehicle for design, so let's review some options.

» Design Council

» Design Teams

» Mindset, Behavior, and Structure Teams

Before we explore each of these vehicles for design, here are two notes to keep in mind:

1. The success of the Cultural Brilliance System is predicated on involvement, input, and feedback from people at all levels of your organization. As you're selecting your design process, please keep that mind. For example, the Adaptogen Design process will not work if the executive team of your company gets together and designs. In fact, this course of action—only asking for the input of your executive team—would hurt your cultural system by breeding distrust and disconnection, the opposite of what you're trying to achieve. But if you've read this far, I'm guessing

that you understand the essence of brilliant cultures and wouldn't do this anyway.

2. By the time Adaptogen Design starts, you know a tremendous amount about your culture—far more than you knew when you started working with the Cultural Brilliance System. You also have a much better understanding of how cultural systems work. Through this new knowledge, insight, and awareness, a potential design may already have begun emerging. Watch for signs of change—seeds you planted earlier in the Cultural Brilliance journey may have begun to sprout.

Design Council

If you are a large organization, you will most likely decide to organize a council to lead the design process. These councils should include representation from all departments and levels of your organization, from the front line to the top line, so that all voices are represented. Remember, as an organization, you're focused on addressing a cultural problem that's emerged and you want to solve it in a way that will decrease stress, inspire learning, and promote organizational health and increase your ability to proactively respond to change.

Design Councils have a large job because, to succeed, they need to do five things very well:

> » Guide your company through steps one, two, and three of the Adaptogen Design process unless you've designated another group to lead that phase.

> » Develop and execute a communication plan to keep the entire organization informed.

> » Create regular opportunities for those who aren't on the council to give feedback at each step of the Adaptogen Design process, through live town hall meetings, virtual conferencing, or any other live communication vehicles. Surveys tend to work less well at this point—interactive communication is most effective here (even if it's virtual).

> » Stay focused on what's best for the cultural system and the people in it—no turf wars, political maneuvering, or power

struggles. The focus is on creating a brilliant culture. Keep your eye on the prize.

» To that end, develop and agree on a set of guiding principles for bringing out the best in the Design Council. Common principles include creating psychological safety, respecting each other, adopting a growth mindset, bringing your best self to the table, watching for your own blind spots and areas of development, trusting the intelligence of the existing cultural system (what's it trying to communicate), and listening to what you hear. (Look ahead to Chapters 9 and 10 for an overview of culturally brilliant leadership.)

Participating in a Design Council takes a large investment of time, energy, and mental capacity. Members will need to have daily responsibilities reprioritized to achieve the level of participation required for success. Design Councils lead the charge on executing the three steps of the Adaptogen Design process.

Design Teams

Design Teams have the capacity to involve hundreds of people in an organization. Using these teams is an effective way to include as many people as possible in hands-on design during step three. To be successful, Design Teams need:

1. A set of guiding principles for the design process, like bullet-point four in Design Councils above (develop and agree on a set of guiding principles for bringing out the brilliance in the Design Council).

2. A set of design parameters, most likely from the Design Council, and if needed, approved by senior leadership. Design parameters are "guardrails" in the design process that address:

   a. The goal of the design process

   b. Time frames for design implementation

   c. Resources that can be used

    d. Money that can be spent

    e. One or two designated facilitators to guide the Design Session, teach the design process at the beginning of the session, and facilitate the presentation/feedback session after Design Teams finish designing their solutions

    f. The Brilliance and Blocks Chart and other outcomes from the Contextual Emergence transition (mindsets, behaviors, and structures that contribute to your company's success and stop your company from moving forward)

    g. A list of the systems involved, how they interact, and potential leverage points in the system (This gets created in Systems, step two of the Adaptogen Design process.)

3. Ideally, the Design Teams work simultaneously for seventy-five minutes to two hours and reconvene once they've completed a draft of their design. A company might have fifteen teams of six people in a large hotel event room or spread out throughout their office space. Each team is designing an answer to one of two questions that you'll want to customize for your organization:

    a. What solution (or leverage point) will move the cultural system or a subsystem from its current state to a brilliant state (as that's been defined by your organization)?

    b. How can we resolve one of our top five to ten blocks? (Below you'll see SN Controls' lists of blocks as examples.) Each team will focus on resolving a specific block.

4. Each team is allotted five minutes to present its designs to the room. The goal is not to find the best or "right" solution but to witness themes and patterns emerging in the process. Ideally, one or two people are at the front of the room at flip charts, tracking themes and patterns as they emerge from the design presentations. The design presentations start with the key leverage point: a specific mindset, behavior, or structure that will shift the cultural system or resolve the block and then each team describes the cultural design (solution) it developed.

After each team presents, the rest of the participants give feedback for up to ten minutes. I like to the use the "I like, I wish, what if" feedback process from the Stanford Design School.[57] This feedback process emphasizes positive improvement versus an analysis of why an idea won't work.

This feedback process is as simple as it sounds:

> » Likes: What did you like?
> » Wishes: What do you wish?
> » What if: What if we . . . ?

SN Controls' Design Team process

When SN Controls started its design process, it prioritized these six blocks to resolve:

1. How do we think and act like a growing, seasoned company?

2. How do we take ownership for decisions?

3. How do we start having psychologically safe conversations?

4. How do we improve interdepartmental communication?

5. How do we prevent people and process work-arounds?

6. How do production processes get streamlined?

To resolve these blocks, SN Controls designated six teams to design solutions. During a three-hour session, the teams learned the Solution Design Process below, worked the process to develop their solutions, and presented their plans to the larger group for feedback.

Solution Design Process

Assess

1. Is the block you're resolving due to a mindset, behavior, or structure?

2. What systems are causing the block? How do these systems interact with each other?

3. What will leverage the most change in the system?

Solution Design

4. Brainstorm solutions. Challenge yourself to find the simplest solution. Use Occam's Razor.

5. Design a solution that meets people, business, and technical needs.

Planning & Implementation

6. Select your solution and create a plan for implementation.

7. How will people need to think and act differently for your solution to work?

After each team completed the seven-step process, it wrote up the highlights of its solution on flip-chart paper. I specifically asked them to capture the answers to steps three, six, and seven and present those to the room. Then all participants gave feedback in the Likes, Wishes, What ifs format and, as the facilitator, I captured those on flipchart paper. In your organization, you'll need to designate someone to present the Solution Design Process and facilitate the Likes, Wishes, What ifs feedback session. Below are three examples of SN Controls' designed solutions to its blocks. In Chapter 7 on Aware Integration, we'll find out how SN Controls implemented these solutions and what happened when they did.

Design Team 1
How can we think and act like a growing, seasoned company?

The best leverage for change is structure:

- ○ Environment—upgrade technology
- ○ Process—availability of resources, evaluate new business line, prioritize risk analysis
- ○ Organizational Design—Strategic Team (long-term thinking), employer brand

Solution: Develop a Strategic Team to focus on long-term planning

How will people need to think and act differently for the successful implementation of this solution?

Think: Have open minds, accept change, and be forward thinking

Act: Need people on the team, time to collaborate is prioritized, action plan is developed and followed

Feedback

Likes: Long term, will stick, will grow the culture, collaboration, employee brand, quality management perspective, and upgrade technology

Wishes: Keep commitment to meeting, annual budget for committee, collaboration should involve customer inpu

What ifs: CEO/company not on board with vision

Design Team 2

How can we take ownership for decisions?

The best leverage for change is behavior:

- ○ More delegation to people in each department
- ○ Clarify job descriptions
- ○ Schedule weekly trainings within each department
- ○ Don't be afraid to ask, "Do I own this?"

Solution: Management team to meet and develop job descriptions for each department so people will feel comfortable taking ownership of decisions. Conduct daily interdepartmental meeting with managers after morning meeting to delegate daily workload.

How will people need to think and act differently for the successful implementation of this solution?

Think: Be willing to ask, "Do I own this?" and seek clarification when needed

Act: Take ownership based on your job description and defined role, move away from the "if you touch it, you own it" mentality

Feedback

Likes: Meeting after morning meeting, job descriptions, training, delegating to your department, "Do I own this?"

Wishes: Job descriptions written by each employee, people can step up to task without delegation, safe to make decisions without repercussions

What ifs: You could spend less time communicating (analyze efficiency)

Design Team 3
How do we prevent people and process work-arounds?

The best leverage for change is structure and behavior:

- ○ Better communication
- ○ Better defined roles and responsibilities
- ○ Okay to say "no" without offending someone

Solution: Create an org chart with names, roles, responsibilities, and direct supervisors. Form committee to handle implementation (one hour per week until date certain or sooner). Make sure to get buy-in from everyone on completed sets of roles and responsibilities.

How will people need to think and act differently for the successful implementation of this solution?

Think: People must be open to having roles and responsibilities defined, okay to say no and okay to hear no

Act: Must be willing to commit to honoring defined roles and to saying/hearing no

Feedback

Likes: updated org chart, saying/hearing no is okay, better communication, defining roles and responsibilities

Wishes: saying no is *really* okay, more root cause analysis, once roles are better defined—people will take responsibility

Mindset, Behavior, and Structure Teams

If you have a large organization, want to involve more people, or want to spend more focused time on mindset, behavior, and structural leverage points, you can create Mindset, Behavior, and Structure Teams. The Mindset Team explores the mindsets that were identified in Contextual Emergence and discusses the following:

> » Which of these mindsets is the most powerful driver of other mindsets, behavior, and structure?

> » If we changed the most powerful mindset, how would behavior and structure adapt?

> » What are ways we could change that mindset?

And then the Behavior and Structure Teams follow the same process. Typically, the teams present in front of the organization for feedback, in person or virtually, following the same feedback process as the Design Teams. Just like with Design Teams, we look for emerging themes and patterns and key leverage points.

Let's return to Islington-Barrett's design

This company decided to create a Design Council. The Council was comprised of one person from every department in the company, the Director of Compliance, and one person from the executive team. Each department was represented by someone doing daily compliance work. For example, an engineer was on the Council instead of the head of engineering.

The Design Council worked together closely to review the Contextual Emergence outcomes and to determine how cultural subsystems interacted and the results of those interactions. With a thorough understanding, they began to look for a key leverage point. At first blush, it seemed like the mindset toward compliance was the obvious leverage point—an opportunity to change the company's paradigm about compliance. But then they remembered Donella Meadows's assertion that leverage points can be counterintuitive, so they looked at what would happen if they pushed the leverage point in the other direction and didn't comment on mindset at all. They knew that when we tell people they need to change their mindset, it usually doesn't work.

A Design Council member said, "What if we create a council like this for compliance—a strategic team that would come together and discuss key compliance issues from a proactive perspective. We won't even talk about mindset. This council will be charged with being a strategic, problem-solving entity. Instead of sitting talking about what a burden compliance is, this strategic team will solve problems and implement solutions."

The key leverage point was structure. In a beautiful twist of fate, getting buy-in for the Strategic Oversight Team (as it came to be known) required a mindset shift. The design was simple and straightforward: The Strategic Oversight Team would meet monthly to anticipate and resolve important compliance issues. Members or "leads" would include IT, engineering, operations, and compliance. The Director of Compliance would lead the Strategic Oversight Team. On a quarterly basis, executive team members would participate in the meeting. By reconfiguring who solved compliance problems, the thinking was that, over time, compliance would become "work we all do" instead of "an extra chore and burden." The approach to compliance would shift from reactive to proactive, from "putting out fires" to strategic and anticipatory. As we'll hear more about in Chapter 7, Aware Integration, this thinking was accurate, and these changes did occur.

It sounds simple, doesn't it? But like most changes, the process hit a few speed bumps. In most organizations, the speed bumps are comprised of the current cultural system expressing its concerns. While these concerns, fears, or resistance can be frustrating to others, they often serve a temporarily important function: to slow the process down long enough to get buy-in, receive feedback, and double-check facts, assumptions, and designs. Is this design going to get us where we want to go? At Islington-Barrett, the executive team was concerned about expanding compliance responsibilities from the compliance team to the Strategic Oversight Team. The leaders expressed concern that the company would become less compliant if responsibility was co-owned throughout the company.

The Design Council and the Director of Compliance were able to address this concern through a series of conversations. The key points included that the compliance team would maintain the high quality of compliance; by implementing a Strategic Oversight Team, compliance issues would more likely be flagged earlier and resolved more easily; and by making compliance part of "the work we all do," it would get woven into the fabric of the company's culture.

As we'll learn about in Chapter 7, all of this happened—and more. Because Islington-Barrett picked the right leverage point, the cultural systems changed their behavioral patterns. Many changes were organic (the best kind) and rooted in a culture of compliance that was strategic, positive, and focused on possibilities.

At this point, you've developed your cultural design, the set of solutions that will help you move your cultural system from its current state to its brilliant state. Now let's move on to the next transition point in the Cultural Brilliance System—Design Integrity. During Design Integrity, we prototype your cultural design, try it out, and get feedback on it. During the transition, we also address concerns and resistance, and get buy-in for what we're about to integrate into the culture. We'll also begin asking an important question: How do I need to grow and how do we need to evolve to bring the solutions we designed—our cultural design—into brilliance?

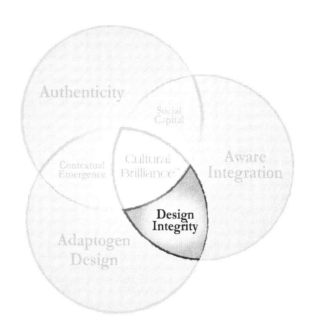

CHAPTER SIX
DESIGN INTEGRITY TRANSITION

DURING THE DESIGN INTEGRITY TRANSITION, IT'S time to take your cultural design out for a test drive. This is an important transitional phase that bridges Adaptogen Design and Aware Integration. During this transition, these questions are answered: Does your cultural design work? Does it achieve the intended results? If it nets a different outcome, what did you learn? What needs to change?

Selecting a small system, such as a team or department, you'll prototype your cultural design (the solutions you designed during the Adaptogen Design Phase), observe how it works, check the logic of the design, and solicit honest feedback. This allows you to paint a picture of success by determining what works and what doesn't and refine accordingly. The art and science of prototyping eases the way for buy-in, accelerates learning, and gives your organization the opportunity to move forward with intention and consciousness.

Prior to the implementation of the prototype, criteria for success are determined based on the original intention of the design. Principles of design thinking guide the introduction of the Design Integrity process.

The leader plays an especially important role in this phase, as s/he stands behind the Adaptogen Design and works with the prototyping team or department to assess the success of the design. During this transition phase, we move out of idea-based designs into the real-world practicality.

In this chapter, we'll focus on these four steps:

Step one: Prototyping: Show, don't tell
Step two: Design the feedback and check for logic
Step three: Revisit the communication plan
Step four: Identify growth and learning requirements

▶ STEP ONE:
Prototyping: Show, don't tell

It bears repeating that how we design the *introduction* of a process is almost as important as the process itself. Because if we don't introduce a process with inclusion, psychological safety, and a willingness to give and receive feedback, there will be very little value in initiating the process at all. As we start the prototyping of your cultural design, it's a good time to revisit your Cultural Safety Zone from Chapter 3, and to clarify the goal of the design you're taking for a test drive.

Let's start by defining what we mean by prototyping. As Rikke Dam and Teo Siang of the Interaction Design Foundation state, "Prototyping is about bringing conceptual or theoretical ideas to life and exploring their real-world impact before finally executing them. All too often, design teams arrive at ideas without enough research or validation and expedite them to final execution before there is any certainty about their viability or possible effect on the target group."[58]

When GE decided to rewire the ecosystem of its worldwide culture, it relied heavily on testing out ideas with employees. GE wanted to create a fast, agile, simplified culture. Design it, try it, learn from it, and iterate it was a modus operandi. Rather than waiting for a "perfect" design to execute, they found that they learned more quickly, raised more employee engagement, and achieved better results through prototyping, learning, and creating the next iteration. They viewed workers as experts on the culture and the design process shaped the data and feedback they were gathering. Part of what has made GE continue to adapt is a willingness to look at things from other perspectives; rather than just seeing what Human Resources sees, Culture Leader at GE Corporate Janice Semper stresses that they've learned to engage with their employees and managers to see what works and what doesn't on their level, continually reevaluating the culture and processes to determine what is working and what needs to be evolved and pushed forward.[59]

In other words, get ready to show rather than tell about your cultural design. Learn by doing. This takes the fear out of jumping in with both feet. Instead of sitting and discussing the cultural design, try it out and discover what you learn. For our purposes, the application of prototyping is straightforward. The steps include

1. Select the prototyping team or department. What group of people is going to try out the cultural design? The team should be comprised of people close to the cultural problem you're addressing or people who experience a high level of impact from it. For example, if your cultural design addresses a plan to give people more autonomy (a requirement of innovation and long-term creative problem-solving), you'll want to pick an intact team or department, such as the engineering department, sales team, or customer experience team—all groups charged with solving problems, identifying solutions, and communicating those decisions back out to other teams.

2. You may also want to select one or two neutral "observers"— people outside that particular team who would sit in on meetings, review outcomes such as deliverables met, problems solved, and other metrics, and share an unbiased assessment of what they've noticed during the prototyping of the cultural design.

3. Identify your time frame. How long will the prototyping last—two days, two weeks, or one month? At what point will you have enough data, experience, and observation to discuss whether the design worked and what you've learned?

4. Design the feedback you want to receive. We'll go into detail on that feedback in the next section of this chapter.

5. Your cultural design embodies mindsets, behaviors, and structures you believe are needed to create a cultural system that proactively responds to change in ways that decrease stress, inspire learning, and promote organizational health. Here's the thing: During this Design Integrity transition, you need to adopt these mindsets, behaviors, and structures because guess what? If you're on the prototype team and your mindset is based on old belief—something along the lines of "this will never work"—you'll be right. It won't work. If your mindset is closer to "I'm excited to try this out, see what we learn, and how we can improve the execution of design," then you'll do that, too.

6. Before you start initiating the prototype, you will want to double-check your cultural design in three ways: empathy, purpose, and coherence of logic. *Empathy:* Does the design meet the needs of the cultural system? Does it meet the stated needs of people in the system? *Purpose:* Is the design congruent with your organizational purpose? *Coherence of logic:* Does the logic of the design hold? Can you see how one step leads to the next? Could you easily explain it to someone else?

And finally, pioneers in design prototyping have identified six common pitfalls to avoid.[60] Let's learn from them.

1. Jumping into the first good idea.

It's certainly easy enough to simply run with what seems like a good idea. Unfortunately, this often doesn't work and prevents you from embracing what may have been better solutions. The truth is, as we learned through the Cultural Brilliance System, most problems are far more nuanced than they first appear, so not giving a solution due diligence can lead to less than stellar "fixes."

2. Getting too attached to your prototypes.

Ownership of a prototype can sometimes cause people or organizations to get too attached to it. Due to that attachment, it can be easy to over-look faults, resulting in the implementation of a faulty model. One way around this, then, is to focus on not trying to perfect your prototype before you test it, which can help limit attachment. Start with quick and fast prototypes with minimal investment and you're less likely to become overinvested in them, making you more likely to see the results clearly.

3. Wasting time pitching or explaining.

Again, it's all too easy to get too invested in an idea or concept, especially if it is yours. Instead, try out an aspect of your culture design and let the results speak for themselves. Don't let perfect become the enemy of better. You can help yourselves do this by building a cultural bias toward action, similar to what Semper noted at GE.

4. Prototyping for the sake of prototyping.

Of course, the opposite can also be true: You can waste time prototyping. Trying out your cultural design is useless if you aren't doing so with a question in mind. You can avoid this by ensuring that whenever you do test a prototype, you have a central question in mind that you are trying to answer. This should also help you keep from getting too invested in your prototype: Remember it is a means to answer a question, and nothing more.

5. Being bothered by failed prototypes.

This is one that organizations and designers can get stuck on quite readily. After all, you've put your time and energy into answering a question, and so it's only natural to be disappointed and/or frustrated when a prototype fails to help you answer that question. But the truth is that failure is its own kind of answer. Learn how you were failing to ask the question correctly, and your next prototype will be far more useful. If you make failure its own learning opportunity, you are far more poised to continue moving forward and evolving.

6. Seeing prototypes as a waste of time.

This, too, is all too common in the corporate world. It's entirely natural for leaders to see the time and energy spent on prototypes and think, "But couldn't we be using that time in other ways?" Sure you could. But doing so would not help you continue to ask the questions that push you and your organization forward. Better to test, learn from the test, and continue pushing forward than to stay stuck in a theoretical framework, which benefits no one and often does become a waste of time. Using prototypes to answer questions allows us to adapt and change more readily and is more efficient in the long term. Spending time on prototypes—which "slow us down to speed us up," as Tim Brown, CEO of IDEO notes[61]—will save you time in the long run.

SN Controls' decided to run two prototypes. The first was a revamp of a production planning meeting they'd been running daily for many years. Over the years, the meeting stayed the same even though the company had grown in revenue, people, and business direction. The company decided that the meeting was no longer effective: It took too long, people weren't getting the information they needed, and attendees were often involved in side conversations. The prototype involved discussions on

> » The most effective people to attend the meeting. Ultimately, it was decided that a representative from each department should attend.
>
> » The information needed by meeting participants. Questions included "What do you want to get out of this meeting? What do you need to know for planning/efficiency? What kind of report do you need?"
>
> » How to rename the meeting in order to reflect its purpose.
>
> » How to design a report that included production stages: Where is each part in the production process? How many days will Quality Control need to test the part?
>
> » Creating a set agenda for each meeting.

After the brainstorming session, the revamped production planning meeting was run daily as a prototype for two weeks. With minor adjustments along the way, participants declared the meeting a huge improvement over the previous version, an improvement that made the rest of their day easier, streamlined communication, and increased their ability to plan.

The second prototype was called a Weekly Review. One work center volunteered to try out the review for a month and then share their findings with the rest of the company. At the end of each week during the trial month, this work center conducted a quick (10–15 minute) review: What went well this week? What did we learn? How can we improve?

After a month, the work center reported that the Weekly Review discussion was valuable. More problems were solved, trust was building, and team work was improving.

▸ STEP TWO:
Design the feedback and check the logic

Before pressing the green light on your cultural design prototype, you have two important steps to complete:

1. Paint the picture of success. How will we know if this prototype works? What are the criteria for success?

2. Design the feedback you want to receive and check the logic of your cultural design.

Painting the picture of success

How will the success of the prototype get measured? I'd recommend identifying no more than *four criteria to determine effectiveness*. For example, Islington-Barrett's prototype was simple: Their Strategic Oversight Team started meeting monthly. They were looking for these criteria as measures of success:

1. Are team members having solution-focused conversations?

2. Are solutions getting implemented quickly and easily?

3. Are the right people in the right conversations?

4. Is the compliance mindset (or paradigm) shifting from "Compliance is a chore and extra work" to "We're all responsible for compliance and it's part of our daily work"?

Islington-Barrett didn't expect that all the criteria would be met in only two or three meetings, but they were listening and watching for the group to trend in those directions. And it did.

SN Controls painted their picture of success by designing the feedback they wanted to receive. Specifically, they selected these questions as their metrics of success for their production planning meeting:

> » Did information flow to the right people and places? The answer needed to be yes.
>
> » How did mindset, behavior, and/or structure change? They specifically wanted to see that behavior changed, that getting the right information to the right people increased the efficiency of the production process.
>
> » Did stress decrease? The answer needed to be yes.

For the Weekly Review, they used these questions as their metrics for success:

> » Was more trust built?
>
> » What did you learn?
>
> » Were you able to more proactively respond to change?

Design the feedback and check the logic

After you've implemented the prototype of your cultural design, it's crucial that you design the feedback you want to receive and check the logic of the design. You'll want to engineer the opportunity for these groups to give feedback: the team involved in the prototype, your observers, and the people in systems impacted by the prototyped cultural design.

A straightforward way to get the feedback process started is to use the Likes, Wishes, What ifs method referenced in Chapter 6.[62]

What did you like about the cultural design?

What did you wish might be different?

What if you tried this instead?

Here are some examples of additional feedback questions to ask:

> » Did you meet your four criteria for success?
> » If not, were the results better than anticipated? Not as expected?
> » How did mindset, behavior, and/or structure change?
> » How did your identified leverage point work?
> » Did information flow to the right people and places?
> » Were the right people in the right conversations?
> » What kind of energy was generated?
> » What did you learn?
> » What needs to change or be revised?

Also check the logic of the cultural design. What did the prototyping process show? Is the design coherent? Can you get from point A to point B easily? Do people understand it? *Is it clear how the design will create the desired result?*

One of the other reasons to prototype, or practice, your design is that circumstances inside and outside your organization will change. We can guarantee that. That's why brilliant cultures are designed to adapt to change. Ask yourself: Does your design allow for growth and evolution? In a 2016 blog post, Seth Godin described this well. Godin talked about a neighbor who had put in a new sidewalk. The workman interrupted the concrete with lines every three feet. Godin then noted, "What are the lines for? Well, the ground shifts. When it does, perfect concrete cracks in unpredictable ways, often ruining the entire job. When you put the breakpoints in on purpose, though, the concrete has a chance to absorb the shifts, to degrade effectively. This is something we often miss in design and in the creation of customer experiences. We're so optimistic we forget to put in breakpoints. There's no doubt the ground will shift. The question is: When it does, will you be ready?"[63]

There's an important breakpoint you'll want to allow for—that old cultural mindsets, behaviors, and beliefs will most likely show up when you least expect them during the Design Integrity Phase. Old ways of being don't necessarily go down without a fight, which makes sense when we remember that how we think and act, and what we believe is tied to our identity. That's okay. You'll want to acknowledge the old ways of being and thinking and remind everyone, without judgment, that new mindsets and behaviors are necessary for your company's brilliant culture to unfold.

Now that you've gathered feedback, learned, and iterated your cultural design, is it ready for implementation? Or do you need to revise your prototype? Do you know enough to move forward with success?

▶ **STEP THREE:**
Revisit the communication plan

You might remember that we discussed the importance of developing a communication plan during the Contextual Emergence transition in Chapter 4. Now is a pivotal time to revisit how you are communicating with those who aren't directly involved in the prototyping process.

It's also a crucial time to capture and communicate what's been learned, what decisions have been made (and how they've been made), and mechanisms for giving and receiving feedback. As part of GE's cultural transformation, the company reconfigured norms around feedback. In GE's culture, feedback had become a stressful word, so it was converted to "insights." It created a simple, yet effective model for providing insights called the Continue/Consider Model—what should someone continue doing and what should someone consider changing? Over time, giving and receiving feedback became an established behavioral norm. Another example of cultivating an opportunity for transparent feedback was the GE's Culture Compass phone app, which allowed employees to see their and others' responses to ten questions on culture in real time. As Semper notes, the Culture Compass "gives us a gauge as to where we are at. It is also meant to be a culture change tool that teams actually use. They can look at the results and ask: 'Where are we making progress? What areas are still challenging for us?'" Even better, it works in real time, allowing GE to continually adapt based on the insights.[64]

People want to be involved, understand what's happening, and help steer the ship. Since they are all part of the daily evolution of the culture, they must be included in its intentional design. A clear, easy-to-follow communication plan is essential.

At this stage, here's how Islington-Barrett's communication plan looked:

> » **Purpose:** We are shifting the culture of compliance from an extra chore and burden to an opportunity for innovation, less stress, and greater integration throughout our company.
>
> » **Picture:** We've designed a new structure for compliance, a Strategic Oversight Team, that will meet regularly to strategically anticipate issues, solve long-term problems, and continue to find ways to integrate compliance practices with less stress. We will prototype the team for three months to determine whether it meets our purpose.
>
> » **Plan:** To prototype the Strategic Oversight Team for three months and to solicit feedback from team members, observers, and others impacted by compliance. Feedback on results, team effectiveness, and the mindset toward compliance will be solicited through a brief survey, individual discussions with each department, and team member experience.
>
> » **Part:** To give thoughtful, astute feedback on the Strategic Oversight Team's effectiveness and how it interacts with your system. If you suggest a change, think about you can lead the change. What's your role in compliance? How can you proactively contribute to a strategic, innovative, less stressful compliance program?

▶ STEP FOUR:
Identify growth and learning requirements

As you've moved through Authenticity, organized and deepened your insight during the Contextual Emergence transition, and developed your Adaptogen Design, you've most likely noticed ways in which people may need to increase self-awareness, expand outside their comfort zone, or allow their identity to evolve. You may also have started cataloging new skills required for new behaviors to emerge. In moments of vulnerability, you may hear someone say that they know they need change, but they're not sure how to make it happen.

Marita Fridhjon, cofounder of CRR Global, shared this perspective on change, growth, and identity: "it indicates that there is movement from the known to the new. I no longer label arguments about the impending/desired/inherited change as 'resistance.' It's simply edge behavior and needs to be normalized. Of course, if you ask me to no longer be the me I have identified with for many years, I am going to fight back! You are asking me to step over the edge into unknown territory and to hang back from that would be normal behavior. Individuals in organizations know what to tackle first to achieve maximum success during change initiatives. All we have to do is provide them motivation and a map from which to make critical decisions." CRR Global cites the "edge" as the line between the known and the unknown, between that which I can identify with and that which poses a threat or difficulty—it is at the "growing edge of what we know, identify and align with in ourselves or our organization. Whenever we try on a new mindset or behavior, we are crossing an edge."[65]

Structured skills development sessions and formal coaching may be needed, especially in larger organizations. In smaller companies, changes may be more organic as people prototype their cultural design and move into the Aware Integration Phase. Sometimes even just discussing the concepts of mindsets, behavior, and structure are enough to alert people to new possibilities.

As you debrief your cultural design prototype, keep note of skills, changes, or new areas of growth required for the successful integration of your cultural design. What do people need to learn that they may need help with? What have they self-identified? Now that you've tested, tweaked, and revised your design, you're ready to transition to the final phase in the Cultural Brilliance System: Aware Integration—where designs become reality and the rubber meets the road.

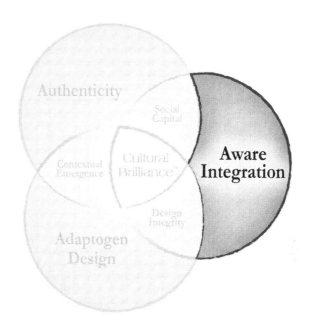

CHAPTER SEVEN

AWARE INTEGRATION PHASE: THE MIND OF CULTURE

BRILLIANT CULTURES EVOLVE IN A STATE OF self-awareness and cultural awareness, which is why the third phase of the Cultural Brilliance System is called Aware Integration. Building on what's been discovered during Design Integrity, this phase moves beyond traditional change management implementation, which is often focused on procedures, tasks, and time lines. During Aware Integration, we emphasize the importance of implementing cultural changes from the perspectives of conscious intention, psychological safety, and systems orientation.

The successful integration of your cultural design will lead to inspired learning, decreased stress, and increased organizational health. As a result, the integration plan is designed by the people who will implement it—incorporating their investment, knowledge, and expertise. The plan includes strategies, solutions, and behaviors aligned with the new cultural system. In this way, the organization develops mindsets aligned with the new cultural system, tells new stories, and builds pathways for positive, complete communication. Simultaneously, the cultural design is continually modified and adapted to respond to both allowances (circumstances in which change flows easily) and constraints (obstacles or roadblocks to change).

This chapter includes strategies, tools, and best practices for integrating cultural changes at the levels of mindset, behavior, and structure. Above all else, process matters. An aware culture knows that the process by which we do something is almost as important as what we are doing.

In this chapter, we'll focus on the three steps of the Aware Integration Phase:

Step one: **Plan preparation**
Step two: **Develop your cultural integration plan**
Step three: **Successful plan implementation**

▶ STEP ONE:
Plan preparation

At this point in the Cultural Brilliance journey, you've probably already seen some iterative changes as mindsets, behaviors, and structures have started to evolve. Before you begin developing your cultural integration plan, you'll want to do three things:

» Assess whether any iterative change has occurred.

» Make sure you implement your plan using new mindsets and behaviors.

» Determine who will lead the development and implementation of the plan.

For the sake of clarity, let's confirm the definition of iteration. According to Merriam-Webster, the basic definition of iteration is "a procedure in which repetition of a sequence of operations yields results successfully closer to a desired result". For our purposes, this means that we'll be watching for ways of thinking, new conversations, or different actions that yield a better, if not brilliant, outcome. These improved results offer evidence that the cultural design you devised works as intended (or even better than intended).

For example, when Islington-Barrett began monthly meetings of its Strategic Oversight Team, the Director of Compliance noticed that those team members were asking different and better questions, such as, "Why do we do this process this way?" "Should we even be doing this process at all?" "How can we improve this process?"

As you might recall, it wasn't easy for the Director of Compliance to get buy-in to form the Strategic Oversight Team. To successfully push "that boulder up the hill," as she described it, she had to help people understand how the team would increase—rather than decrease—the company's compliance. The conversations required for getting buy-in opened the door to new ways of thinking, and people began to ask questions that replaced the former refrain of "We don't have time," "We're too busy," and "I just need to put out today's fire."

Here are key places to watch for or confirm changes, shifts, or evolutions in the cultural system:

> » Are people thinking or acting differently? We know your cultural system is evolving when people behave differently. To behave differently, and have it stick, most people need to change their thinking, or mindset, as well.
>
> » Do you hear different conversations? Maybe the content or the tone of conversation has evolved into more positivity or possibility seeking (versus venting about problems and feeling disempowered to solve them).
>
> » Are you hitting points of resistance or tension? If you are, it's worth exploring further. Mindsets and behaviors that no longer serve the organization often resurface with intensity as the system and the people in it try to maintain behavior that's known and comfortable. If this happens, you'll want to address it head on through direct, compassionate conversation.
>
> » Has the cultural system or a subsystem changed its behavior? As we discussed in Chapter 5, Adaptogen Design, systems

themselves have set patterns of behavior until a leverage point alters the pattern.

» What has already evolved, changed, or improved? You'll want to document those shifts in your plan because people are not always aware of subtle or minor changes. Knowing that change is occurring energizes people and gives them hope and momentum.

Before you create your cultural integration plan, I'd like to emphasize a critically important concept: **You must integrate your cultural design from the perspective of the new mindsets, behaviors, and structures.** You cannot implement change using old mindsets, behaviors, and structures. This is an example of the Cultural Brilliance System's iterative nature: The act of implementing your cultural design will, in fact, move you closer to the culture you desire.

For instance, if a company decides to build a psychologically safe cultural system, they'll want to implement a cultural design that shifts people's behaviors into a zone of psychological safety. If, however, the team sits down to their first planning meeting and engages in a discussion that further frays trust and leaves people feeling defensive and guarded, how can they possibly integrate that cultural design? To be successful, they need to have a conversation that addresses questions like these:

» How will they determine if they feel psychologically safe? What are signs, feelings, and behaviors?

» How can they create a psychologically safe team?

» How will they share feedback with each other?

» At the beginning of each planning meeting, ideally, they'll reaffirm the answers to these questions. They'll notice how the cultural system is evolving (or not) and what their cultural intelligence is telling them.

As a final preparation step, be sure to decide who will develop your plan and who will lead its implementation. Many organizations decide to establish a Cultural Integration Planning Team. This team focuses on determining the best ways to integrate the cultural design into the existing cultural system and then plans out the implementation of the design. If you decide to use a planning team, be sure that they are given time and space to focus on the planning and implementation process. Otherwise, they will have competing priorities and daily work may overtake their planning efforts. Because planning team members are invested in the process, they also make excellent "cultural ambassadors"—enthusiasts who are early adopters of change, new mindsets, and new behaviors.

▸ STEP TWO:
Develop your cultural integration plan

Now that we've outlined crucial areas of awareness—noticing iterative change, integrating your design with new mindsets, behaviors, and structures, and identifying who will develop and lead the implementation of your plan—it's time to look at the structure and organization of your integration plan. But before you do that, here are questions for your planning team to consider:

1. What do we *functionally need to do* to integrate our cultural design? Also, what practical coaching, training, or skills-building will people need to do to be successful and aligned with the new cultural design?

2. Are we primarily working at the level of mindset, behavior, or structure? What's the leverage point we're using?

3. What's the communication plan, and how will we get regular feedback?

4. How will we know the cultural design is working?

Now let's delve into each one of these questions to find what is most important to understand, do, or learn.

*What do we **functionally need to do** to integrate our cultural design? Also, what practical coaching, training, or skills-building will people need to do to be successful and aligned with the new cultural design?*

The answers are often practical ones because we're talking about strategic action planning. It makes sense to review your cultural design (and the solutions within it) and make a list of new mindsets, new behaviors, and new structures/systems. From there, start to identify which solutions are easiest to implement. Do you have quick wins? How about low hanging fruit? Which changes will require more planning, time, and buy-in? If you have a new mindset you'd like to instill throughout your company, what are creative ways to accomplish this? How can you create excitement and enthusiasm for these changes?

Make a list of all conversations, tasks, and any processes that need to be handled. Note what's already accomplished, changed, or evolved. You'll also want to identify coaching, training, or skills-building that needs to be arranged. Then identify who is responsible for completing each item by what date and how they'll communicate the outcome.

This process doesn't need to be complicated and definitely doesn't require a twenty-five-page plan. Ideally, you'll capture this information on a few pages or a few slides. The mantra throughout the cultural integration process is "simple and thorough." What's the straightest route from point A to point B? Complexity is sometimes viewed as a mark of intelligence in companies. Don't make that mistake; don't get mired in complexity. Simple, elegant, straightforward solutions will help ensure your success. Remember Occam's razor: The simplest solution is usually the best one—and the correct one.

Islington-Barrett's Director of Compliance created a few slides that contained their cultural integration plan. The first slide articulated the contrast between the current culture and their preferred brilliant culture. Slide number two gave a brief overview of the Strategic Oversight Team's purpose, their goals, and the role of individual team members. The third slide outlined a simple, yet specific meeting agenda. This agenda was a modified version of a holocratic meeting agenda.[66]

The Director of Compliance was committed to running the Strategic Oversight Team meeting differently than other meetings at the company. She believed, correctly, that the different agenda would encourage a new mindset and would also signal that these discussions were, in fact, meant to be strategic, focused, and solution-oriented. Here's a sample meeting agenda:

» Two minute "hot topic" round

» Review last meeting's slides

» Identify topics for future meetings

» What are upcoming risks?

» Other issues?

» Discuss current compliance work

» What else?

Additional slides outlined the long-term objectives of the Compliance Department and how and when the Strategic Oversight Team would meet these objectives. This chart also addressed how feedback would be received and results would be communicated throughout the larger organization.

SN Controls' cultural design included creating a psychologically safe work environment. To accomplish this, the company recognized that it needed to teach people the mindsets, behaviors, and skills of psychological safety. The CEO met with the company to develop a set of guidelines for developing a psychologically safe environment. Then the company held a series of weekly training sessions. Training and discussion topics included handling emotional triggers, giving and receiving feedback, having safe conversations, learning from mistakes, ownership and empowerment, and the power of perspective.

Are we primarily working at the level of mindset, behavior, or structure? What's the leverage point we're using?

You already know the answer to these questions. You simply want to remind organizational members what you're doing and why. Remember, you've designed, prototyped—and redesigned, if needed—based on feedback. You're not changing anything at this point. Just make sure to state your answers in your plan. One or two sentences will suffice.

Here's an excerpt of the initial plan that SN Controls developed. This company used the leverage point of ownership/empowerment as the basis for the rest of the plan.

Introduction to cultural integration plan

The primary leverage point to address the six "blocks" is **ownership/ empowerment (two sides of the same coin)**. This plan integrates solutions developed by the six Design Teams.

Blocks

» How can we think and act like a growing, seasoned company?

» How can we take ownership for decisions?

» How can we have psychologically safe conversations?

» How do we improve interdepartmental communication?

» How do we prevent people and process work-arounds?

» How do we streamline production processes?

Ownership in the workplace means you are accountable for your responsibilities. It also means that you step up to solve problems and help others when you can.

Empowerment is the authority or power given to you to do something. It's important to try new behaviors, ideas, and processes for about a month—tweaking and adjusting as needed. Change takes time and can feel temporarily uncomfortable. It's helpful to give things some time.

Ownership/Empowerment Behaviors—for Everyone

> » Make a good faith effort to **arrive at a solution** or bring a solution to a manager (if an okay is needed).
>
> » **Avoid the "you touch it, you own it"** mindset and behavior. If you are asked to help or offer to help, make sure you clarify whether you can assume this responsibility. **If you are only agreeing to help that one time, clarify that, too.** Further the conversation by suggesting a way to handle the task going forward.
>
> » Avoid participating in a work-around. **Kindly redirect someone if they want to work around someone else by coming to you.** It's okay to say and hear no.
>
> » If it's unclear who will assume a task, ASK this question, **"Who's going to do this?"**
>
> » At the end of week, each work center does a **quick (10–15 minute) review:** What went well this week? What did we learn? How can we improve?
>
> » At company meetings, share what your **work center is learning and improving.**
>
> » If you need to solve a problem, **call a meeting or a 10-minute conversation** with people who can help you solve it. Share your solution with the right people.

Tasks to Complete

Process or Task	Due Date	Owner
Conduct psychological safety discussions and create a list of expectations and guidelines.	6/29/18	Jasper
Incorporate walkie talkies. Jasper is testing sample communication devices.	In process now	Lily
Create a public calendar for meetings. Everyone will be able to schedule and change meetings.	6/29/18	Ralph will work with IT company
Reactivate training documentation in production.	6/29/18	John and Lily
Post "Idea Board" (white board) in Break Room.	6/29/18	Lily
Update and post coverage chart.	6/29/18	Jasper will update and post
Meet with small production teams to gather ideas, concerns, and feedback.	7/15/18	Claudette
Clarify/realign roles and responsibilities.	7/15/18	Claudette leads
Create more detailed org chart.	7/27/18	Strategic Team
Organize long-range planning team.	7/27/18	Susan, Lily, and Peter
Training on active listening, safe conversations, eliminating blame and gossip (mini-trainings during company meetings).	9/1/18	Susan

Process or Task	Due Date	Owner
Increase delegation in each work center.	Immediate	All managers
Create a presentation describing how SN Controls' products are used— connect daily tasks to the big picture.		Eric and Lisa
Get product to Shipping & Receiving the day before it ships (use Root Cause Analysis to uncover and resolve glitches at each point in production process. Look for the simplest solution). Solving this will require resolving other production issues.	Finish Root Cause Analysis by 7/29/18. Determine next steps.	Jasper (lead), Jim, Eric, Geneen, Louise, and Bob
Initiate and complete both prototypes: Production Status Meeting and Weekly Review.	7/29/18	Claudette will organize Production Planning Revamp meeting; Bob will lead review (see below)
Assess all progress around 8/1 and revise as needed.	8/1/18	Claudette leads
Continue to review and build out plan on a monthly basis: As these tasks are accomplished, the next set of steps will emerge.	Ongoing	

What's the communication plan, and how will we get regular feedback?

During the Aware Integration Phase, you'll want to update your 4 Ps[67] plan as follows:

Purpose: Why are we designing a new culture? What problem are we solving? What are we trying to accomplish? People often need to understand the logic of a change before they can change, especially within a cultural transition. *What you're trying to accomplish may be different than originally envisioned. By engaging in the Cultural Brilliance System your purpose may have naturally evolved.*

Picture: What is the endgame? How is it going to work? What is evolving and what isn't? People often need to imagine what the new cultural system will look like before they can give their hearts to it. *Be sure to update your picture with the revised cultural design that you're going to integrate.*

Plan: What is the road map for getting to where we need to go? What is going to happen over the next X months? What happens first, second, third? *Be sure to update your time line and next steps. Most likely, timing and next steps have changed due to what you learned from prototyping your cultural design. You'll also want to include the time line for the Aware Integration Phase.*

Part: What is my role? How will I be involved? Do I have an opportunity for input into the plan? When will I be trained? What's the optimal mindset for me to adopt during the process? People need a tangible way to contribute. *Again, here you'll want to update how individuals will be involved. People who have specific identified roles should be noted, too. Clarity and transparency are the names of this game.*

Depending on the cultural design you're integrating, your communication plan may be quite simple—in fact, the simpler the better. If you are a larger company, you may need a more detailed communication plan to ensure that people feel included, are kept in the loop, and understand how they can give feedback. Islington-Barrett and SN Controls used existing company communication channels, such as regularly scheduled town hall meetings, staff meetings, and digital forums. In fact, Islington-Barrett noticed that once the Strategic Oversight Team began meeting, communication started to cascade organically as team members reported back to their own departments.

SN Controls' created a communication plan focused on how each individual person could contribute to the company's success as its cultural system evolved.

SN Controls' Culture Change Initiative: Understanding Your Role

> » **Purpose:** To help SN Controls design and implement a cultural system that allows the company to adapt to change more easily, to decrease everyone's stress, and to increase learning and ownership. These changes will create an environment in which people can enjoy the company's growth, innovate more easily, and solve long-term problems.
>
> » **Picture:** We'll keep all the best parts of the SN Controls' culture, such as trustworthiness, high quality, integrity, positive energy and good humor, caring relationships, responsiveness to customers, and engineering precision. We'll resolve the communication and productivity bottlenecks that are causing stress and holding people back from speaking up, innovating, and solving problems.
>
> » **Plan:** At the beginning of June, the Cultural Implementation Team will meet to plan implementation of the solutions you designed. Once the plan is completed, you will receive it and have a chance to offer feedback.
>
> » **Part:** Offer feedback on proposed changes. Challenge yourself to try new things. Ask yourself questions, such as
>
> - Do I own this?
> - How can I help create an environment in which it's safe to have direct conversations, take ownership, and execute ideas?
> - How does what I'm doing affect another part of the company? Who needs this information?
> - If asked to participate in a work-around, say "no" and suggest that the person communicate with the appropriate person.

SN Controls' cultural integration plan also included vehicles for communication and feedback. As you can see, the company decided to keep communication and feedback mechanisms simple and straightforward. A larger company or company with multiple geographic locations would most likely use digital formats for communicating and gathering feedback.

Communication Plan

> » Weekly email updates (will also be posted on company bulletin board).

> » Give 10-minute updates at company meetings (over the next few months as new ideas and processes are implemented). People giving updates should rotate based on what's happening in the company.

> » Create a chart to mark the progress on a white board.

Gathering Feedback

> » Create a suggestion and feedback box.

> » 10-minute update/discussion at company meetings.

> » Generate periodic survey.

> » Small group conversations (Small groups every 6-8 weeks to gather feedback on what's working, what's not working, and what's changed).

Your organization can receive feedback through face-to-face conversation, digital means, or a combination of both. Depending on the size of your company, I usually suggest a combination. Digital options can include online polling, online chat rooms, and surveys. For example, the technology company Zeal provides company leaders with a suite of check-in and measurement tools to provide consistent and accurate metrics of company morale and culture. Information is collected by a fun and personable AI, a "chatbot" named Ava, who interacts with employees. She conducts check-ins at regular intervals and delivers data and analytics to talent managers and executives, providing the information they need to build an engaged workforce and positive company culture.[68] Nothing replaces an open, honest discussion that starts with "How's it going? What's working and what isn't? What are your suggestions for improvement? What's emerging? What are we learning?" Especially in larger companies, a technical solution, like Zeal's, can help to grease the wheels of an open feedback conversation.

No matter how you decide to receive feedback, your response to that feedback is a crucial trust building, "listening" moment. If you ask people for feedback, you need to acknowledge you've received it, let them know how it will be used, and act on the feedback (when possible). Companies build trust by showing that asking for feedback isn't just a token gesture.

How will we know the cultural design is working?

As you're developing the cultural integration plan, you want to answer this question as clearly and simply as possible. Qualitative or quantitative metrics will work here. As discussed throughout the book, we don't know that a cultural system has evolved until we witness that people think and act differently and begin to get better business results. The key is to identify three or four key metrics based on your original cultural goals. "We'll know our cultural solutions are working when we see X, Y, Z . . ." Keep watching for what's emerging in the system, notice when people change their behavior, and watch for any signs of people or systems getting stuck, bogged down, or overly stressed.

SN Controls decided on an initial set of behavioral indicators to help them determine the success of their cultural design:

> » People are more open to change and fail fast.
>
> » Getting the right people in the right seats decreases stress.
>
> » People are speaking up and asking questions.
>
> » Focus on the process, not the person (changes, mistakes, and misunderstanding are not personalized).
>
> » The environment feels psychologically safe to the people who work there.
>
> » Products get to shipping department the day before the ship date.
>
> » 98 percent on-time shipments.

▶ **Step three:**
Successful plan implementation

As you implement your cultural integration plan, consider the importance of these principles, actions, and perspectives.

- » **The introduction of the change is consciously designed.** This means that once you've constructed your cultural integration plan, you design its introduction. *Important questions to answer include* How will you roll out the plan? Will you have a company meeting? Town hall meetings? Meet with individual departments and teams? How will people give feedback on the plan? How will you ensure that everyone feels that they are important participants in the plan implementation process? How will you galvanize energy, enthusiasm, and excitement for what's about to happen?

- » **Organize your Cultural Integration Team.** In most organizations, this team is needed to guide implementation and harness positive energy around changes in the cultural system. This team will need to have time specifically dedicated to this purpose so team members can bring energy, ideas, and their best thinking to the project.

- » **Momentum matters in this phase.** In fast moving cultural systems, a temporary slowing down to be deliberate and thoughtful is often effective. In slower moving, entrenched systems, the opposite is often the case: A faster implementation pace can energize the organization, especially if you work with early adopters and allies of the cultural change. This is a judgment call because you don't want to move so quickly that you create resistance. Look for pockets of enthusiasm and positive energy and start there. For example, engaging people who haven't, historically, had as much of a voice in the company can jumpstart change.

- » **The plan respects people and honors their dignity as human beings.** People are acknowledged for their contributions, efforts, and individual brilliance. As mentioned in the previous section of this chapter, a clear communication plan, including a feedback system, is initiated.

- » **The implementation of your plan models new mindsets, behaviors, and structures.** A successful integration of your cultural design will forward your company's purpose and profits.

» **Watch for old mindsets, behaviors, or structures to surface with intensity.** This resurgence can reveal itself through, for example, conflict, power-keeping behaviors, or gossip/blaming, and there can be a tendency to think you're heading in the wrong direction. While reaffirming the plan is always a good idea, most likely you're dealing with old mindsets and behaviors rising to the organizational surface that need to be addressed. Since much of a cultural system's dysfunction arises from unconscious assumptions that hinder the culture, it's not uncommon for the surfacing of old mindsets and behaviors to seem like an unexpected "slap" from the cultural system. At this point, you'll want to ask people to use their cultural intelligence to notice what's happening. You'll want to address these situations head on and reemphasize the new organizational direction.

» **Responsive and positive communication is emphasized at every step.** Questions like "What are we learning?" "What are we noticing?" "What's emerging?" are asked at regular intervals. When people have questions or concerns, these issues are addressed in a responsive way. Temporary confusion, hesitancy, or questioning is expected as you deploy your plan.

» **Ownership for aspects of the plan is clearly delineated.** Time lines are identified and project management strategies and tools are employed as needed. Follow-through on plan implementation is just as important as communication. If for some reason you can't follow through on a commitment made to the organization, communicate that clearly, transparently, and quickly.

» **Completion of one initiative or task may organically lead to another one.** Witnessing this evolution is a positive outcome of the plan implementation. Both Islington-Barrett and SN Controls experienced this iteration.

In the next chapter, Social Capital, we'll focus on assessing the success of your cultural integration, as well as discussing ways to keep your cultural system evolving in its own brilliance. As we look to this final transition in the Cultural Brilliance System, we want to keep these commitments in mind: the trust and truth embedded in psychological safety, the courage to be brilliant, and the understanding that mindsets, behaviors, and structures have their own logic. As you deploy your cultural integration plan, a final word: Don't let emotion cloud your judgment, and simultaneously, remember that empathy is just as important as analysis.

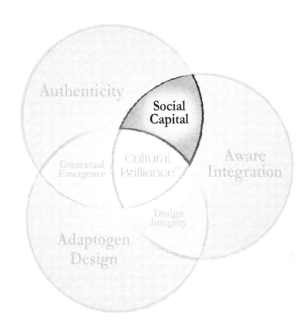

CHAPTER EIGHT
SOCIAL CAPITAL TRANSITION

BY THIS STAGE OF THE PROCESS, YOU'RE ON YOUR WAY
to integrating your redesigned cultural system. Over the next weeks
and months, you'll watch the brilliance of your culture emerge in new
and varied ways. As this evolution continues, it's an opportune time to
check in and assess how your cultural system has changed and what
your organization has learned. In the Cultural Brilliance System, we
call this final transition Social Capital. Why that name? Social capital
is a form of cultural and economic capital in which social networks are
central, marked by reciprocity, trust, cooperation, and a focus on the
common good.[69] When cultural systems become brilliant, they do so, in
part, because self-awareness and systems awareness have increased. This
evolution of awareness can only occur and continue through trust, open
communication, and intentional action.

When an Adaptogen Design is successfully integrated, it inherently builds trust, encourages truth, and creates an environment of respect. A culture can't be brilliant unless it's rooted in psychological safety. As we learned throughout our Cultural Brilliance journey, organizations iterate their brilliance by engaging in truth-based dialogue that allows people to share what they experience, sense, and observe. We can't be brilliant without this form of social capital, especially when we want to decrease stress, inspire learning, and promote organizational health. During the Social Capital transition, your company assesses how it's evolved, what it's learned, and whether you've have met your goals. Building on that assessment, we then shift focus to learning how to stay brilliant.

In this chapter, we'll focus on these two steps:

Step one: Assess how your cultural system has evolved

Step two: Learn how your cultural system stays brilliant

▶ STEP ONE:
Assess how your cultural system has evolved

During a series of conversations, we ask questions that focus on business results and learning. Sometimes, at this point, there's a temptation to skip this step, in the name of "saving time" or "everyone already knows our outcomes." Social Capital discussions increase awareness through self- and organizational reflection. People aren't really aware of what and how much they have learned until they reflect on it and discuss those outcomes. The Social Capital transition is a form of continuous improvement. Typically, companies will conduct the Social Capital conversations three to six months after the initial implementation of the cultural integration plan.

A study conducted by David Zes at the Korn Ferry Institute underscores the importance of this step. As Zes notes,[70] more self-aware companies are also more profitable, as a 2013 Korn Ferry study proved quite illustratively. In particular, the research team looked at nearly 7,000 self-assessments from professionals at nearly 500 publicly traded companies to identify "blind spots" in leadership, then used those results to compare the performance of those publicly traded companies. By this point, it probably shouldn't surprise you to hear that more self-aware companies outperformed less self-aware companies. In fact, poorly performing companies' workers showed fully 20 percent more blind spots—and were a whopping 79 percent more likely to have low overall self-awareness, reported Korn Ferry. Given that stock performance was also tracked for a full thirty months as part of the study, this wasn't just a fluke. Instead, we now know that companies with more self-aware employees—where people have more social capital at their disposal—significantly outperform companies with less social capital.

When Islington-Barrett, for example, conducted their Social Capital check-in, they were glad they did. So much had changed for the better in a few short months that they hadn't recognized and internalized all of it. Once the company's Strategic Oversight Team gained traction, mindsets shifted from "compliance is a burden that's someone else's problem" to "compliance is everyone's responsibility." People regularly approached the Director of Compliance with new questions, insightful ideas, and process improvements. "What can we do to help everyone?" evolved as an underpinning of the culture of compliance. "This is work we do" instead of "extra work" was the new mindset.

Accordingly, conversations changed, too. Instead of "we don't have time," the new discussion included questions like, "Why are we doing it?" "Should we be doing it?" "If we're going to keep doing it, how can we improve it?" This line of questioning increased strategic thinking and allowed the team to define problems more accurately.

Because Islington-Barrett had such high standards for compliance, the Strategic Oversight Team questioned whether they were going above and beyond. In response, the Director of Compliance created a flow chart that each department could use to assess the strength of their internal controls. If a department was able to show that they met the standards outlined on the flow chart, they were exempt from submitting an annual compliance assessment—a huge savings of time, energy, and effort for that department. Meeting these standards also reinforced the exact behavior desired by this culture: Compliance is part of everyday work and is everyone's responsibility.

Another result was a shift in Islington-Barrett's executive team's perspective. They got involved and enthusiastically supported the initiative. These leaders observed that when they participated in partnership with (rather than managing) the Strategic Oversight Team, they could help ease the organizational burden in significant ways.

When I asked the Director of Compliance what allowed them to achieve these results, she emphasized the importance of the Authenticity Phase of the Cultural Brilliance System. The team reported that they felt deeply heard during the cultural assessment phase, and the Director said she really listened differently during that process. Additionally, the Adaptogen Design Phase gave them the opportunity to see their system in a fresh way. Best of all, the company's trust level increased throughout the culture of compliance. People reported feeling safe enough to speak up when they had a compliance issue, pushing critical information directly to the Director and Strategic Oversight Team.

So you can clearly see why this final check-in is important.

Conversational tools and structures

As you begin the Social Capital process, don't forget to reestablish the Cultural Safety Zone, if needed. Depending on the size of your company, you can conduct this discussion in a variety of different ways. A face-to-face conversation is always best—if your organization is large, organize a series of department discussions, focus groups, or integrated team conversations. Just like during the Design Integrity transition, create or continue digital opportunities to share successes, results, and new opportunities for change through online forums and feedback systems like Zeal (described in Chapter 6, Design Integrity Transition). Remember why this transition is called Social Capital. You want to invite and coach people to continue to notice the cultural intelligence, to speak up about concerns and opportunities, and to point to signs that a cultural pattern or behavior is changing.

Once you've decided on how you'll conduct your Social Capital check-in, you want to decide which questions you'll use to discuss business results and learning. What follows are examples of questions you can use to harness the energy of the Social Capital transition.

Business results: What have we achieved?

Consider the following questions:

> » How have business results improved? What's the impact?
>
> » How would you describe the quality of your relationships, trust, and communication? What's the impact?
>
> » How has stress decreased?
>
> » How has learning increased?
>
> » How has organizational health improved?
>
> » How well do we proactively respond to change? Has this ability become a competitive advantage?
>
> » What allowed us to achieve these results?

Learning: How have we evolved?

Consider the following questions:

> » What have we learned about ourselves?
>
> » What have we learned about our cultural system?
>
> » What's emerging in our culture? What's the energy like?
>
> » How well do we listen to ourselves and to each other?
>
> » What's our mindset?
>
> » What behavioral changes do we see?
>
> » What allowed us to achieve these results?
>
> » What's the most profound outcome of this experience?

SN Controls selected three questions from the "learning list" and three from the "business list" and polled their company. People met in small groups first to discuss the questions and then forwarded a list of responses. These responses were compiled and shared during a company meeting. During the meeting, the importance of tracking what's been learned was revealed. SN Controls realized they'd achieved far more than they had anticipated. Several meeting participants noted how they had grown as individuals. The company made the popular decision to use the Social Capital inquiry quarterly to gauge progress, learning, and areas of opportunity. They also noticed new mindsets, behaviors, and structures that were emerging in their culture and followed up on that energy to implement new ideas, solutions, and coaching opportunities for individual development.

▸ STEP TWO:
Learn how your cultural system stays brilliant

Once you've assessed how your cultural system has changed, teams and departments will want to consider how they can stay brilliant and continue to proactively respond to change. I've created a dialogue-based process for doing just that, the Adaptogen conversations. This dialogue is designed to help organizations continue to recognize, and resolve when needed, issues, growth, and iterations in their cultural systems.

Integration of change in many organizations is considered static once it's complete. "Well, that change is implemented. We're all done!" This is always a mistake because, as we know, cultural systems are dynamic, fluid, and adaptable. Because of this, they are almost always in a state of opportunity. Here's what I mean: Systems, unless they are very stuck, are usually available for learning, insight, and greater awareness that can lead to their next positive iteration.

An iteration, or evolution, of your cultural system could be improving how the sales team communicates with the product development team—it doesn't need to be dramatic or appear far-reaching. Often a subtle change in the behavior of a cultural system will have lasting positive or negative impact. That's why it's so important to be aware of your cultural systems and subsystems, and what's trying to change within them. Often unintended consequences, such as the Challenger example in Chapter 3, are put into play because people don't know how to observe the signals in the cultural system, they don't believe it's safe to speak up, or their mindset has created a blind spot.

What follows is a process—the Adaptogen Conversations—that you can use to teach self-awareness and systems awareness, to anticipate and resolve issues in ways that evolve the brilliance of your culture, and to integrate those insights, changes, or actions. Remember that brilliant cultures are adaptogen—they naturally seek balance and want to "right the ship" when the organizational steering goes off-kilter. Small problems are easier to fix than large problems, so let's catch them early.

The adaptogen conversations

As we know, brilliant cultures proactively respond to change in ways that decrease stress, inspire learning, and promote organizational health. Once you've implemented your cultural integration plan and started to get feedback on how it's working, you'll want to begin to shift your focus on how to stay brilliant. One of the best ways to do that is to teach people how to engage in Adaptogen Conversations. As you may recall, adaptogens help systems rebalance, grow, and thrive. Since cultural systems are dynamic, not static, we want to make sure they evolve in ways that benefit your organization. These conversations can occur on a team, between two people, or within an entire organization. They can last ten to fifteen minutes or three hours, or anything in between.

The Adaptogen Conversations are designed to help you spot small problems before they become big problems, to notice what's happening in your cultural system, so you can anticipate problems, and to surface tensions, relationship issues, and positive trends. Engaging in dialogue at the level of energy, heart, and head takes people out of the day-to-day and asks them to stop long enough to notice what's going on both inside and outside themselves.

Decrease stress: The energy conversation

In this first conversation, we use our cultural intelligence to discuss what we're noticing. For example, are unexpected problems cropping up? The goal here is to anticipate changes in relationships and systems. In other words, if something feels off, it probably is. The cultural system may be giving signals, such as a sudden rash of mistakes, an unusual conflict, or a drop in morale. Or you may sense an uptick in new ideas or passion for an innovative direction and you want to harness that positivity. Conversations include broad questions such as

> » What do we know and what do we sense, observe, or feel?
>
> » What's the energy like in this group?
>
> » What's slowing down in the company? What's accelerating?
>
> » What's emerging or changing (in the company, in departments, or on teams)?
>
> » How do we need to realign?

Inspire learning: The heart conversation

Now that we've tuned into the energy and identified what might need attention organizationally, we explore these areas through listening, curiosity, and generating possibilities. Before jumping to a solution, we take the time to listen to ideas, insights, and concerns, with an eye toward the cultural system. Conversations can include questions such as

> » What's our level of trust right now? Do we need to enhance psychological safety?
>
> » What relationships, systems, or processes need attention?
>
> » What's happening throughout the culture?
>
> » How are systems operating? How are people behaving? How is the culture evolving?
>
> » What are ideas for resolving this issue?
>
> » What mindsets, behaviors, or structures need to be accessed or created?
>
> » What did we learn? How will we incorporate and broadcast this learning?

Promote organizational health: The head conversation

Now it's time to decide on a course of action. Building on what's already been discussed, what data, facts, or information do you need (if you don't already have them)? In this conversation, you want to be practical, identify your solution, and develop a plan of action. Conversations can include questions such as

> » What do we need to make an effective decision in this situation?
>
> » What are our solutions and next steps?
>
> » How do our next steps align with current mindset, behaviors, or systems?
>
> » What's the plan—both action plan and individual roles? How will it be communicated and implemented?

What's the outcome of these conversations? On the surface you're most likely resolving a problem, but what you will find that, over time, a deeper learning and increased awareness emerge from these conversations. You can use the Adaptogen Conversations, the Social Capital learning and business questions, or create your own process. Each time you focus your conversation at the levels of energy, heart, and head, you weave a new level of inspiration into the culture that reenergizes its positivity, invention, and iterative growth.

In Part Three, Culturally Brilliant Leadership, we shift our focus to the unique role of the leader during the *Cultural Brilliance* journey. While it's clear that the success of this process rests, in part, on the inclusion of people from all levels and areas of your company, leaders have an influential role. Next, we'll learn how leaders can skillfully guide their organizations through the Cultural Brilliance System.

Part Three

Culturally Brilliant Leadership

INTRODUCTION TO CULTURALLY BRILLIANT LEADERSHIP

IN PART THREE, WE SHIFT OUR FOCUS TO EXPLORING the leader's role in initiating, designing, and integrating a brilliant culture. Although the participation of all organizational levels is undeniably important in the evolution of a brilliant culture, a leader's mindset and behavior will either catalyze or drain your cultural system's brilliance. As a leader, you have two choices. You can either lead the charge, while mounted on a horse, carrying your white flag, and inspiring people to grow into the best versions of themselves. Or you can drain the energy from the system by treating people unfairly, being unwilling to tell the truth about your culture, and keeping your blinders firmly in place.

If you've read this far, you're probably choosing the former. Good for you. The world needs leaders who are willing to grow brilliant cultures. We need leaders who are willing to ask the questions, "How am I shaping our cultural system today?" and "What's the next iteration of our brilliance?" and "Why are we stuck?"

Culturally brilliant leadership entails a heightened level of self-awareness, a connection to the "right brain" of a culture—relational aspects such as trust, creativity, and emotional risk-taking. This doesn't mean we the leave the logical, linear, transactional part behind, instead we seek a balance. Culturally brilliant leaders can use both sides of their brain for the benefit of their culture.

The culturally brilliant leader's critical role is to align motivation, energy, and cultural systems throughout the Cultural Brilliance System. Your role is to give meaning and context to what's happening throughout the process. Culturally brilliant leaders help to harness the organization's emotional energy to catalyze the system to move forward, and throughout the process, leaders and followers begin to see that their cultural systems—at the levels of mindset, behavior, or structure—can be aligned with a company's purpose, strategy, and goals.

Consider these hallmarks of culturally brilliant leaders:

> » These leaders lead and role model learning. When mistakes are made or a process breaks down, they ask the question, "What if this is a learning problem, not an execution problem?"
>
> » They are keenly aware that their actions build trust and that doing what they say they are going to do matters.
>
> » They recognize that they themselves need to continue to grow, develop, and evolve. As a shepherd of the culture, it's part of their responsibility.
>
> » They know they have blind spots and that they can't see their entire cultural system clearly because no one person can see an entire system.
>
> » As realists, they are willing to tell hard truths because if they don't, no one else will.
>
> » They recognize that culture isn't a thing off to the side that we take out and dust off every few months. To that end, they shape cultural systems with intention and inclusion.
>
> » They have respect for people, as well as their potential, and hold them accountable for high performance standards.

As an example, when Market Basket, a supermarket chain in New England, fired long-time, beloved CEO Arthur T. Demoulas in 2014, employees protested heavily. They did this because Demoulas had supported them in a unique way: Not only did he offer his employees company-wide profit-sharing and better-than-average benefits and pay, he was kind to them, too. And when workers were at risk of not receiving bonuses from the profit-sharing plan after the 2008 financial crisis, Demoulas put money from his own pocket back into the plan, so that people would still receive their bonuses. His actions built trust and galvanized loyalty, and that in turn brought his workforce together—to the point that they were willing to protest his ouster.[71]

In the next two chapters, we'll explore how a leader can become a "culture whisperer" and use that ability to harness the positive emotional energy of a cultural system.

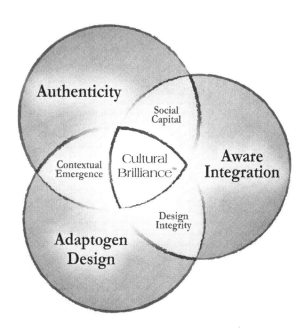

CHAPTER NINE

BECOME A CULTURE WHISPERER

THE MOST CULTURALLY BRILLIANT LEADERS BECOME culture whisperers in their own right. Just like a horse or dog whisperer, leaders—or really, anyone in a culture—can learn to tune in, sense, and observe what might be happening in an organization. Culture whisperers learn to read the signals that their cultural system is in trouble through tell-tale signs like missed shipments, a flare-up of conflict, or suddenly ineffective decision-making.

On the road to becoming a skilled culture whisperer, leaders often discover that they are prone to occasional bouts of "culture blindness"—an inability (or unwillingness) to see a reality in their cultural system. In this chapter, we'll unpack how culture blindness creeps up on leaders and how a Cultural 360 Process—which we'll examine in more detail shortly—can help leaders return to greater awareness of themselves and the cultural system.

Culture whisperers also leave people in a place of learning rather than a place of defensiveness.[72] So often leaders inadvertently leave people in a place of defensiveness after an interaction. Even if they don't mean to, many leaders inadvertently address their team members in a way that puts them back on their heels rather than lifting them up. Luckily, culturally brilliant leaders recognize that the best way to help people grow is to leave them in a place of learning, connection, and trust.

In this chapter, we'll focus on

> » Recognize and cure culture blindness
> » Leave people in a place of learning

Recognize and cure culture blindness

Culture blindness refers to a leader's blind spot about an aspect or reality of the cultural system. While culture blindness may be constant or temporary, it usually stems from a leader's lack of awareness of his or her impact, the current state of the culture, or how others are playing a role the leader doesn't see. It can be challenging for most of us to see our direct impact on a cultural system. While it's true that culture transforms as mindsets, behaviors, and systems evolve in an organization, the leader often has an important hand—real or perceived—in shaping the culture, promoting its real or espoused values, and setting the stage for the growth or stagnation.

As an example, many leaders are hired because they are decisive and take action. While talented in these areas, some leaders may not understand the complex reality of change. When leaders view change as only a procedural or task-oriented process, they go blind to a cultural system's needs during a change. A CEO can't lead an organization through a change without realizing that the cultural system will either allow the change or make it as easy as fitting a square peg in a round hole—and that the change requires buy-in, emotional intelligence, and a healthy communication strategy. Nor can a leader decree that a culture is going to be innovative or force a new collection of values on a team. At the end of the day, culture wins.

Another common form of culture blindness is the assumption that people don't have emotions at work, or, if they do, they shouldn't show them. This blindness is akin to saying that people aren't human, but rather robots, when they come to work. People do their best work when they can bring their whole selves to work.

These are examples of being blind to the reality of a cultural system. Culture whisperers don't make these mistakes very often because they know that truth, trust, and psychological safety are the Holy Grail of brilliant cultural systems, and that becoming blind to an aspect of a cultural system will only erode trust over time.

Even culture whisperers, though, may miss a beat in the organizations they lead. Consider these signs that you're not seeing everything you need to see:

> » People or processes start to feel out of sync. This can initially be a "sixth sense" that something just isn't right. It may be hard to put your finger on this feeling. What normally works well stalls or even grinds to a halt.
>
> » You feel like you're pushing a boulder up a hill. Sometimes you need to shoulder that boulder and the cultural system is better for it, but unexpected challenges are a symptom that you'll want to investigate.
>
> » People seem unusually stressed, tense, or angry, but you can't point to a particular cause.

If you're concerned you might be suffering from a bout of culture blindness, the Cultural 360 Process can help regain your foothold on your cultural system. A Cultural 360 is a communication process any leader can facilitate to gain a better understanding of their organization, of any blind spots, and how specific issues are perceived. The steps in the 360 are simple.

Cultural 360

1. Invite individuals from all areas/levels of your organization to participate. From whom do you need feedback on this issue? Make sure to include people that have different vantage points.

2. Explain the purpose of the conversation and how information will be used. The leader communicates how feedback will be collected, how it will be used (e.g., to learn and grow as a leader), and how the results will be shared. There should be no negative consequences for telling the truth. Make sure participants know if you will share the compiled feedback with them (and the company as a whole, if applicable).

3. Establish confidentiality and welcome their candid feedback.

Ask a series of questions, such as

> » How does our culture shine?
>
> » How does our culture hold us back at an organizational or individual level?
>
> » What am I not seeing about our culture, or myself, that I should be?
>
> » How could we better align our culture with our business direction?

It's highly likely you'll want to customize and narrow these questions to elicit the feedback you need. The Cultural 360 framework is flexible and should be tailored to fit your specific needs. You can initiate it as a formal set of interview questions, or as a series of quick discussions with a few people when you need to check-in on what you're observing in the cultural system.

One leader I worked with, Raul, was caught in an extremely tense relationship with Peter, a key player on his senior team. Raul and Peter led a division of a major insurance company. Although a talented professional, Peter seemed chronically unhappy at work and that emotion colored how he interacted with people. As an accomplished culture whisperer, Raul noticed that his team member's unhappiness was shifting the relationships on their team. Determined to better understand Peter's dissatisfaction, Raul invited him to meet for lunch a few times over a period of a few weeks. Although this wasn't an official Cultural 360, Raul used the same principles, by asking Peter questions about the root cause of his dissatisfaction, what he thought Raul should be seeing but wasn't, and how their team's cultural system was impacting Peter.

After two lunches, Raul began to understand that Peter felt frustrated and angry about a new team dynamic. Peter believed that Raul had gone blind to the behavior of two team members, Stacey and Ben, who were engaged in a personal relationship outside the office. Raul had decided to handle the news of this personal relationship by ignoring its potential impact. Inadvertently, Raul and the rest of the group he led had allowed a "pink elephant" to show up: the dynamics of the personal relationship were causing tensions to run higher on the team. Peter, who worked most closely with Stacey and Ben, was deeply affected by these tensions. Once Raul realized his role in Peter's and the team's unhappiness, he addressed the situation directly with Ben and Stacey. Together, they agreed on a set of boundaries to keep the personal relationship out of the professional setting. Then Ben and Stacey met with the team to apologize and explain their plan for holding better boundaries at work. Peter, who was immensely relieved, began to enjoy a much easier relationship again with Raul. Raul is a great example of a leader who leaves people in a place of learning—another important element of being a culture whisperer.

Leave people in a place of learning

"Leave people in a place of learning rather than defensiveness." When my colleague Hugh McGill, organizational change and cultural development practitioner, mentioned this concept to me,[73] its simplicity and wisdom struck me deeply. Hugh has a history of helping manufacturing facilities successfully transform their cultures. In tandem with working with team members on the production floor, Hugh coaches senior leaders to get to know the people on the production floor and, during conversations, how to leave them in a place of learning.

Often without realizing it, leaders leave people in a place of defensiveness by criticizing them, blaming them, and making them feel "less than." Inadvertently, they create conditions that erode psychological safety and trust. While it's true that some leaders want to instill fear in the people that work for them, in my experience, most leaders don't realize the negative impact they sometimes have on others. Leaving people in a place of defensiveness can stem from a leader's blind spots, a "one-size-fits-all" approach to communication, or his or her own stress, to name a few cata-lysts. Rajkumari Neogy, a pioneer in the field of neurobiology of inclusivity and belonging, the creator of the Disruptive Diversity coaching frame-work, and the author of *The WIT Factor: Shifting the Workplace Paradigm by Becoming Your Optimal Self,* says that when we judge (or criticize or blame) others, we do so to preserve and protect ourselves.[74] Our judgment of other people, a situation, or a conversation is an unconscious attempt to create safety for ourselves in that moment. If I judge someone for a decision they made, I get to stay "safe" in my rightness that the other person is wrong. Again, this process is almost always an unconscious one that we can bring more awareness to noticing over time.

Here's a list of common behaviors that leave people in a place of defensiveness:

1. Not listening to what you hear or not listening at all

2. Interrupting people and interrogating them

3. Needing to be right

4. Being hard on others' decisions

5. Criticizing them

6. Not trusting people; lack of delegating

7. Creating a psychologically unsafe environment

8. Creating a culture in which people are afraid, disrespected, and disengaged, then complaining about those people and blaming them for a lack of performance

Unfortunately, this list of behaviors is all too familiar. Most of us have experienced being on the receiving end of many of these behaviors, and we know firsthand how they damage truth-telling, psychological safety, and learning.

Fortunately, culture whisperers know that leaving people in a place of learning is as much a mindset as it is a set of behaviors. We need to change how we think and act to accomplish a conversational exchange of that caliber. Leaving people in a place of learning includes mindsets like these:

1. Be open to what you hear, to differing views, and to the idea that you don't have all the answers.

2. Be willing to let go enough to allow others to take risks.

3. Be vulnerable enough to learn and share that learning.

4. Be open to connecting via a mutually respectful adult-to-adult interaction (instead of a top-down manager to direct report interaction).

As leaders, we want to engage in dialogue with the goal of building trust and connection, a dialogue that forwards our learning and the other person's as well. Leaving people in a place of learning is mutual. As a leader, you can learn just as much as, if not more than, the team member with whom you're speaking. To begin, you check your ego at the door and remember that if you want others to take risks, share ideas, and be willing to learn, you need to model this by using skills and taking actions like these:

> » Listen and get curious: Ask good questions.
> » Be honest, tell the truth, and hold people accountable.
> » Trust people's abilities, decisions, and problem-solving.
> » Help people grow, ask what they've learned, and find out what they need.

When leaders model these behaviors and "walk their talk," they set the stage for harnessing their cultural system's emotional energy—the heart of brilliant cultures. We'll delve into these mindsets and behaviors in Chapter 10.

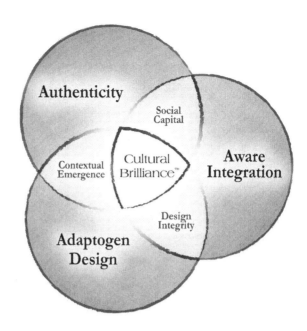

CHAPTER TEN
HARNESS YOUR CULTURE'S EMOTIONAL ENERGY

THE SKILL OF HARNESSING YOUR CULTURE'S EMO-tional energy isn't listed in any leadership job description I've ever seen. Yet, like Arthur T., Market Basket's beloved CEO, that's what many effective, respected leaders do. They inspire people, rallying them around a vision and giving them an opportunity to contribute to something greater than themselves. What's rarely discussed is how they tap into the positive emotional energy of the culture and galvanize it for the greater good. Whether they know it or not, these leaders attend to the cultural system and instinctively figure out what will move it forward. Usually keen observers, they may watch for leverage points in the system, as outlined in Chapter 5, to understand its behavioral patterns. These leaders have the courage to see what's possible in people and the culture, and almost always have great respect for both. They understand that people need to trust their leaders, their intentions, and their actions.

How can you harness the emotional energy of your cultural system? As a leader, you represent the hub of the organizational wheel. Your job is to exhibit these mindsets and practice these behaviors: to listen, to create a psychologically safe and inclusive environment, and to guide your company through the discomfort and/or exhilaration of growth at pivotal cultural evolutions. To do that you need to understand your company's reality—with this information you can harness the behavior of your cultural system by understanding the mindsets and structures driving the system's behavior.

To support your ability to harness your cultural system's energy, let's learn more about the key skills that will support your efforts: listening to what you hear, uncovering your blind spots, and considering the ideas, concepts, and actions outlined in the leadership checklist.

In this chapter, we'll specifically focus on how to

» Listen to what you hear

» Shine the light on your blind spots

» Use your leadership checklist

Listen to what you hear

Just as children engage in selective hearing, so, sometimes, do leaders. We often listen to what we want to hear or hope to hear, while closing our ears to what we don't like. I stumbled upon this idea a few years ago when I participated in a community choir, the kind in which you don't need to audition, but do need to attend 95 percent of rehearsals to continue to participate. One night at rehearsal, the choir director, a very experienced professional, said, "For the rest of the evening, please focus on listening to *what you actually hear* as you sing." His request hit me like a bombshell as I realized how often we don't listen to what we actually hear.

How does this relate to cultural systems and leadership? When you begin to listen to what you actually hear—whether you like what you hear or not—you can change your behavior based on this new information. Let's say the head of purchasing comes to you, raises an issue with a vendor, and you dismiss it because you are having an extremely stressful day. What will happen then? If the head of purchasing needs your input to handle the situation and you're not willing to listen, nothing happens. Most likely, the unresolved issue will cause your company to incur unnecessary expense, the head of purchasing will get frustrated, and others in the supply chain won't have the materials they need at the right time.

What if you do listen fully, despite your high stress level? The issue has a high likelihood of getting resolved, you increase trust and safety with the head of purchasing, and the supply chain isn't held up. This is a simple example and it's one that is happening every minute of every day in almost all organizations.

Below are five questions to self-assess how well you listen.

Questions for self-reflection

1. *Do I stop myself from deciding in advance what people are going to say?* This isn't a good idea. No one can truly predict what someone else is going to say, and when we do, we're no longer listening in any meaningful way.

2. *Do you listen with a mindset of curiosity?* When people listen with a mindset of judgment, they're more likely to respond with closemindedness, defensiveness or blame.

3. *Do I actively seek ideas, knowledge, and perspectives different than my own?* Am I willing to not know the answer to everything during a conversation?

4. *Do I manage my stress so that I can still listen?* After all, if our stress gets too heightened, we can't effectively listen.

5. *Do I listen to what I hear?* That is, do I really listen, and listen fully?

To be a culturally brilliant leader, your answers to these questions are ideally all yes. Don't worry, though, if you have some honest no's because you can change your listening style. Simply practice listening to what you hear, be curious, and begin seeking out new ideas and perspectives. Keep an open mind and try to refrain from anticipating what people will say before they say it.

Here's the thing: All people in a cultural system deserve to be heard, especially the ones you don't want to hear. People with unpopular viewpoints often have an important message to convey. For example, I was consulting for a technical design company and one of the engineers had been labeled a bully. It was true that his communication style was harsh and critical. He was not an open-minded listener and wasn't particularly interested in others' views. However, his business acumen and engineering know-how were almost always accurate. While that doesn't excuse his negative impact on others, it does point to the reality that even challenging voices—and sometimes especially challenging voices—often flag important issues in the cultural system that need to be addressed.

When you listen to what you hear, you allow a dialogue to emerge, problems to get solved, and learning to occur. The Director of Compliance at Islington-Barrett said that, in retrospect, she was solving the wrong problems. When she started listening to what she was hearing, she was able to get to the root of the compliance issues more accurately. Even the most well-intentioned leader can fall prey to believing that they understand the root cause of a problem, simply because from their vantage point, their problem definition makes sense.

When leaders listen to what they hear, they go a long way toward creating psychologically safe, inclusive work environments. To that end, psychological safety is an organizational state of being that extends beyond trust: It's the belief that you won't be punished unduly if you make a mistake. That's not to say you won't be held accountable (after all, accountability is a foundational part of trust), but that your team and colleagues will still support you and won't value you less because you made a mistake. Numerous studies have demonstrated that psychological safety improves creativity, helps people better speak their mind, and allows for more moderate risk-taking behaviors—all the sorts of things that can lead to major breakthroughs.

I discussed these ideas with Rajkumari Neogy. She said, "Leaders can think they're doing everything right and could still offend someone."[75] While culturally brilliant leaders are accountable for their self-awareness, Neogy raises an important distinction—we are not responsible for other people's reactions. We can be picture-perfect and someone having a bad day could still take offense. If that happens, how do we handle it? Neogy outlines an approach she calls "rupture and repair": When there's an emotional rupture, we need to work to repair it with the other party.

A rupture could result from someone having that bad day, getting emotionally triggered, or not feeling seen, heard, and valued. Neogy also says that one of the best ways the brain can change its perceptions of what has happened is through language.

When we really think about this, it makes sense. Without conversation—an exchange of facts, feelings, and listening—emotional repairs don't happen in safe, inclusive ways. When we apologize, it doesn't mean we're admitting we're wrong. It simply means we want to repair the rupture—the damage done through a communication, perception, or interaction gone wrong. A leader can go a long way toward repairing a rupture by saying, "It seems like something isn't right between us. I'm concerned that I've miscommunicated. Can we sit down and talk? I'd like to listen and learn from you." Culturally brilliant leaders have these sometimes difficult but usually worthwhile conversations.

What stops us from listening fully and repairing ruptures? In short, our blind spots.

Shine the light on your blind spots

Everyone has blind spots. But a leader's blind spots seem to shine more brightly than others' and that light gets magnified throughout the culture. A blind spot is a mindset, belief, or behavior of which we are not aware. Most of the time, everyone around us sees our blind spots clearly because blind spots are a repeated pattern of behavior, often the result of an unconscious bias, such as needing to be right or being overly risk averse. Blind spots develop, too, when a leader makes an inaccurate assumption about someone and acts on that assumption, without checking it out first. Here's a simple example. If a person in your organization is repeatedly late for a job that requires a specific start time, you might assume the person isn't very committed to the company or their job. If you act on that assumption without first verifying its accuracy, you're acting, literally, from the blind spot of not having accurate information. Culturally brilliant leaders know they have blind spots and use them as opportunities to increase their self-awareness.

How do we shine the light on blind spots? By asking for feedback, by seeking to understand how our thoughts and actions impact others, and quite simply by asking, "What am I not seeing that I should be seeing?"

When I discussed leadership blind spots with Stephen Shambach, a retired Army Colonel with forty-five years of leadership experience in military, civilian, and academic organizational settings, he shared these blind spots and ways to increase self-awareness:

1. *Inaccurate self-image.* Often leaders will have an overly optimistic perception of themselves. **Remedy:** Ask for feedback on how you are perceived.

2. *Underestimating the importance of communication.* **Remedy:** Ask someone working at a lower level in an organization—on the front line, or in the field—if they understand the organizational mission, vision, and direction. If that communication has reached them clearly, you're doing a good job. If not, find out where the breakdown occurred and what's needed to improve communication.

3. *Not setting priorities when everything is important.* Especially now, everything seems important in organizations. Without prioritization, though, people are directionless, and their stress levels increase when they don't know what to do first. Although this may seem obvious, leaders don't always understand the impact of not setting priorities. In these situations, people report feeling yanked in different directions as priorities rotate. This results in wasted effort, mutual disappointment, and a potential decrease in trust and commitment. **Remedy:** Analyze your priorities and select the one that makes the most impact. Once that has been addressed, you can then move forward to the next priority. Give people a road map to follow.

4. *Not being authentic, especially when mistakes are made.* It's true that most people dislike admitting mistakes when they make them, yet when a leader attempts to cover up a blunder, he or she sets the tone for the entire culture to do the same. **Remedy:** Candidly acknowledge your mistake(s), what you learned, and how the error(s) will be remedied. Normalize vulnerability and transparency.

5. *Not listening for accuracy and understanding.* As we discussed earlier in this chapter, listening isn't only registering that someone is speaking. Sometimes leaders don't listen well because what they hear doesn't align with their worldview. **Remedy:** Seek out those who do not share your perspective or viewpoint. This may help reveal a blind spot. Listen to what you hear. If it doesn't align with your perspective, this may be important information for you to have. You can't change what you can't talk about.

Rosemary Strunk, JD, a Gallup Certified Strength-Based and Presence Coach, says, "If you want to change the culture, change yourself."[76] To the extent that you can increase your self-awareness about your blind spots and your impact as a leader, you will absolutely shift your mindset about your culture, which will change your behavior and how you interact within the organizational systems. As Rosemary and I took a deeper dive into blind spots and how they affect us, she made a key point: People can't eliminate every blind spot. We can only shine the light of awareness and make better and different choices once we become aware of a blind spot.

It's also worth noting that some blind spots are generated by two autonomic biases. These are survival-based, hardwired biases: the confirmation bias and the negative bias. The confirmation bias explains our tendency to want to be right. The certainty that we are right allows us to take decisive action. Thousands of years ago, our survival depended on this ability. The negative bias results in a predisposition to assess risk and avoid it when possible. Again, estimating the risk in a situation paved the way for longer survival. Both biases were survival instincts and when we view them this way, they not only make sense, they explain why some leaders avoid risk, sometimes in seemingly unnecessary ways, and some leaders take action, sometimes seemingly too quickly.

Harold was the CFO of a large software company. In many ways, he was a capable leader who cared about his team, but like many leaders, he kept stumbling over a few blind spots. The biggest one was rooted in the confirmation bias: a strong need to be correct in all situations. When Harold engaged in the process of exploring this blind spot and its impact, he realized that he believed if he admitted an error or made an incorrect decision his job would be in jeopardy. If his job was in jeopardy, his survival could be imperiled, thus the blind spot. Like most blind spots, Harold's made sense once he recognized his behavioral patterns—behavioral patterns such as criticizing or blaming others when they disagreed with him, a rigid adherence to the organizational hierarchy, and not listening well. Fortunately, Harold finally received the feedback and support he needed to change his behavior and the underlying beliefs creating the blind spot. If he hadn't been able to shift his behavior, he most likely would have lost the job he was protecting. In essence, Harold was walking down a path to a self-fulfilling prophecy. Luckily, this job loss was averted.

How can you make sure your blind spots don't trip you up? Rosemary Strunk shared four simple strategies:[77]

1. Generate five different perspectives. When the outcome matters, stakes are high, or there's tension, look at the situation from five perspectives and see how your viewpoint changes with each one.

2. Ask for feedback from people you trust who are different from yourself and will be honest with you. Here's a good question to use: What do you think I should be seeing that I'm not seeing?

3. Be curious and present. Inquire and seek to understand others from the perspectives of mind and heart. Be attentive and notice how others react to you. You don't know what you don't know.

4. Be sure to know your strengths. An awareness of our strengths increases overall self-awareness. When we undervalue our strengths, we create more blind spots in ourselves (by not seeing what's true about us), and we lose the opportunity to empower others. If a leader downplays their strengths, they will likely downplay others' strengths, as well. Correspondingly, if we overuse our strengths, new blind spots get generated there, too. An overused strength reminds me of the saying, "If all you have is a hammer, everything looks like a nail." A common example of an overused leadership strength is achievement. While an achievement-oriented leader is often quite successful, they sometimes overuse that strength by trampling others' thoughts, feelings, and ideas on their quest to achieve a goal.

By understanding your individual and cultural blind spots, listening to what you hear, and leaving people in a place of learning, you are much better equipped to lead your company's journey through the Cultural

Brilliance System. Here's a checklist to help you stay centered, focused, and aligned with your cultural intelligence.

Use your leadership checklist

What follows are ideas, concepts, and actions to keep front and center as you lead your cultural evolution. Some will resonate more than others, but all are worth taking under strong advisement. I've seen talented, determined, caring leaders falter because they overlooked one or more of the items on this list.

1. **Support.** What support do you need as you navigate in uncharted cultural waters? Many leaders hire coaches or consultants to partner with them through the process. The basics of stress management, sleep, and nutrition are important to consider, too.

2. **Leadership Impact.** Do you have a clear understanding of how your leadership has impacted the current cultural system? Both the Cultural 360 Process and the Authenticity Phase of the Cultural Brilliance System can help you gain a deeper, more accurate understanding of your impact. Your blind spots may shade an accurate perception of your full impact. When in doubt, ask your organizational members, colleagues, and trusted advisors for feedback.

3. **Team Growth.** Everyone on your leadership or executive team will need to learn, grow, and evolve. You cannot lead change without changing yourself. Some leaders make the grave mistake of thinking that only the people working in their company need to change. Nothing could be further from the truth, which segues into the fourth item on this list.

4. **Role Modeling.** New mindsets and behaviors must be modeled by you, your leadership team, and those implementing the cultural change. Otherwise, people won't trust and won't buy into organizational changes.

5. **Go Deep Temporarily.** As we've seen, the Authenticity Phase and Contextual Emergence transition are both deep dives into

the inner workings of your cultural system. It's helpful for you and for others in your organization to know that this depth is temporary. We're diving for treasure, but we'll come up for air in the Adaptogen Design Phase.

6. **Courage.** You need to be a courageous listener and truth teller. If you try to work around a person, situation, or problem, you will lose the trust of your followers. Listen to what people tell you, investigate if needed, and take action as appropriate. If your star performer is messing with your culture, trust me when I tell you that you probably don't need them.

7. **Tough Conversations.** You also need the courage to have tough conversations. You might need to give feedback, you might need to address someone's resistance, or you might uncover a saboteur. SN Controls' CEO had to address resistance to change at regular intervals.

8. **Cultural Blow ups.** The parts of the culture that no longer serve the organization, the blocks, most likely will "show up and blow up" at an unexpected point in the process. It's challenging to predict, and your organization will weather it. Almost always, I find that "blow ups" (conflicts, irrational behavior, working against the process) are opportunities to address important issues that have been lurking underground.

9. **Challenges.** Some phases of the Cultural Brilliance System will be more challenging than others. When this happens is different in every company. Stay the course—sometimes it will be a grind and then the tide will turn.

10. **Flexibility.** Be willing to change the cultural integration plan if needed. Keep prototyping, get feedback, and fail fast.

11. **Identify Your Allies.** Seek those who fully support your cultural evolution. Make them cultural ambassadors, communicators, and doers. Make them visible and give them credit. One of SN Controls' early allies was a talented, long-time production

supervisor. He helped to galvanize the support of the manufacturing floor.

12. **Message, Communicate, and Make Meaning.** Leaders have a rare opportunity to make meaning. You can shape the context of your organization's cultural change by how you communicate, the stories you tell, and the actions you take. Communicate key messages early, often, and more than you think you need to.

Above all, let ideas, trends, and patterns emerge in the system and keep following them. That's your gold. Notice what's emerging and pay attention to it. Trust that one iteration will lead to the next in the most beautiful, challenging, and unexpected ways. Watch as your culture's brilliance reveals itself.

EMERGENCE

Many books end with an epilogue, no doubt a fine way to end. To stay in alignment with the iterative nature of Cultural Brilliance System, we're going to conclude our journey together, not with an epilogue but with an emergence.

The root of the modern word *emergence* is the Latin root "emergere," which means "to bring to light"—in fitting alignment with cultural brilliance. Every step along our path to this point was designed to cast a glow on the potential, invention, and intelligence in your people and in your culture.

In modern, organizational speak, emergence happens when a cultural system disrupts its own behavior and coalesces into a new form or behavioral pattern.

Let's retrace the steps of your culture's emergence. We discovered that brilliant cultures are organizational systems that proactively respond to change in ways that decrease stress, inspire learning, and promote organizational health. With that in mind, we learned that cultures operate in systems of mindsets, behaviors, and structures that sequence in patterns that drive communication, decision-making, and results. It also became clear that truth, trust, and psychological safety are the elements that ignite brilliance in culture. Without the courage, heart, and conviction to tell the truth, we can't do much of anything and, absent those cultural changes, our organization will remain mediocre.

We moved on to understanding that brilliant cultures are inherently adaptogen (adapting and producing). Adaptogen designed cultures evolve into brilliance as they perceive change not as something to be resisted but as something to be embraced differently. Adaptogen designs ensure that cultural systems can rebalance themselves as they adapt, learn, and grow. But to accomplish that, they need to integrate their designs—the solutions to cultural problems—with intention, awareness, and planning.

Insights included self- and systems awareness coupled with the recognition that we cannot become brilliant without listening to what we hear, leaving people in a place of learning, and getting feedback on our blind spots. In other words, our cultural systems can't be brilliant without raising collective consciousness. Toward the end of our journey, your organization pinpointed what had emerged and how your cultural system had evolved.

Listen to what wants to emerge in your culture and yourself and act on it. That's really what cultural brilliance is about. With that ability to notice, give voice to, and act on a flame that's been sparked, you can change yourself, your company, and the world. It's not always easy to follow the heat of that flame, but the effort is worth it.

What's emerging for you? What's emerging today in your cultural system?

Listen. Allow the emergence. Be brilliant.

ACKNOWLEDGMENTS

Thanks so much to Kenneth Kales, Sheri Hanlon, and the team at Waterside Press for their professionalism, attention to detail, and caring. It's been a pleasure and privilege to work with them.

Bill Gladstone is a wonderful agent and human being. I feel extremely fortunate to have him represent my work. Harry Pickens, coach extraordinaire, helped me tap my own brilliance and reconnect with myself when I couldn't figure out what was next. Dr. Pat Baccili and the Transformation Talk Radio (TTR) team are huge supporters of my work. An extra special, heartfelt thanks to Dr. Pat for mentoring me through launching the *Cultural Brilliance* brand, coaching me as I wrote the book proposal, and for countless conversations about cultural brilliance. Jesica Henderson, Linda Firing, and the rest of the TTR team are responsive, smart, caring professionals.

I am immensely grateful to Melanie Holden and Lisa Campion, both tremendous supporters of me and my work. Lisa introduced me to Bill Gladstone, an introduction that changed my life. Melanie gave expert editorial feedback on the entire book, offering game-changing suggestions and support. Thank you from the bottom of my heart for these amazing gifts.

While I was writing this book, I had the pleasure of partnering with a wonderful editor, Matt Stebbins. Thanks to Matt for his enthusiasm, his research, and his great editing. Additional thanks to Kerri Stebbins who read and gave key feedback on the book.

Deirdre McEachern has believed in me for the past fifteen years of our weekly coaching exchange and I appreciated her friendship and support throughout the book writing process. Carol Alexander and Mike Matchett read early book chapters and shared valuable feedback, enthusiasm, and editing.

With deep appreciation, I thank and honor my clients for their courage, willingness to change, and belief that culture can be brilliant.

I also thank Dylan and Sarah for being a part of my family.

None of this would mean very much without my husband, Tim Walsh, and my son, Ethan. Thank you so much for your love, support, and humor. You are my heart.

ENDNOTES

Cultural Brilliance System: Step-by-Step

1   *Adaptogens: Herbs for Strength, Stamina, and Stress Relief*, courtesy of David Winston and Steven Maimes (Rochester, VT: Inner Traditions/ Bear & Company, 2007).

Chapter One

2   Edgar Schein, *Organizational Culture and Leadership*, 3rd ed. (San Francisco, CA: Jossey Bass, 2004).

3   Tim Kuppler, Culture University (www.cultureuniversity.com).

4   Michael Schneider, "Google Spent 2 Years Studying 180 Teams. The Most Successful Ones Shared These 5 Traits," Inc., July 19, 2017, https://www.inc.com/michael-schneider/google-thought-they-knew-how-to-create-the-perfect.html.

5   "The Neuroscience of Trust," *Harvard Business Review*, January–February 2017, https://hbr.org/product/the-neuroscience-of-trust/ R1701E-PDF-ENG.

6   Workplace Bullying Institute, "Estimating the Costs of Workplace Bullying," April 24, 2014, www.workplacebullying.org/costs/.

7   Amy Edmondson, "Building a Psychologically Safe Workplace," TED video, https://www.youtube.com/watch?v=LhoLuui9gX8.

8   Terrie Lupberger is a coach and advisor to senior executives, as well as a former CEO. Her website is www.terrielupberger.com.

Chapter Two

9   Otto Scharmer and Katrin Kaeufer, *Leading from the Emerging Future: From Ego-System to Eco-System Economies* (San Francisco, CA: Berrett-Koehler Publishers, Inc., 2013), www.bkconnection.com.

10 Christopher Kline, "A Deep Dive into the Cultural Brilliance of the Markelle Fultz Letter," FanSided, June 24, 2017, https://thesixersense.com/2017/06/24/philadelphia-76erscultural-brilliance-markelle-fultz-letter/.

11 Edgar Schein. *Organizational Culture and Leadership*, 3rd ed. (San Francisco, CA: Jossey Bass, 2004).

12 Excerpt(s) from THE FIFTH DISCIPLINE by Peter M. Senge, copyright © 1990, 2006 by Peter M. Senge. Used by permission of Doubleday, an imprint of the Knopf Doubleday Publishing Group, a division of Penguin Random House LLC. All rights reserved.

13   John Pourdehnad, Erica R. Wexler, and Dennis V Wilson, "Systems
      & Design Thinking: A Conceptual Framework for Their Integration"
      (paper, 55th Annual Meeting of the International Society for the
      Systems Sciences, 2011), 807–821.

14   Joseph C. Calitri, "The Pursuit of Very Goodness: Corporate Social
      Responsibility" (presentation, American Cyanamid Company, Princeton
      University, Princeton, NJ, April 26, 1979).

15   Excerpt(s) from THE FIFTH DISCIPLINE by Peter M. Senge,
      copyright © 1990, 2006 by Peter M. Senge. Used by permission of
      Doubleday, an imprint of the Knopf Doubleday Publishing Group, a
      division of Penguin Random House LLC. All rights reserved.

16   Ibid.

17   Ibid.

Chapter Three

18   Seth Godin, "Defining Authenticity," personal blog, http://sethgodin.
      typepad.com/seths_blog/2017/10/defining-authenticity.html.

19   Global Human Capital Trends Report, Deloitte University Press,
      www2.deloitte.com/content/dam/Deloitte/global/Documents/
      HumanCapital/gx-dup-global-human-capital-trends-2016.pdf.

20   Cynthia Forstmann, Theresa Agresta, Andrea Cotter "The CultureTalk
      Survey," www.culturetalk.com.

21   David Krueger, MD, is an Executive Mentor Coach, and CEO
      of MentorPath®, an executive coaching, training, publishing, and
      wellness firm. More information about his work can be found at www.
      mentorpath.com.

22   Reprinted with permission of the publisher. From *Humble Inquiry: The
      Gentle Art Asking Instead of Telling*, copyright 2013 by Edgar Schein.
      Berrett-Koehler Publishers, Inc., San Francisco, CA. All rights reserved.
      www.bkconnection.com.

23   Henry Petroski, "Failure Is Always an Option," Op-ed, *New York Times*,
      August 29, 2003.

24   Pat Salgado, "Changing Organizational Culture from a Liability
      to an Asset," The Systems Thinker, https://thesystemsthinker.com/
      changing_organizational_culture_from_a_liability_to_an_asset/.

25   Report of the Presidential Commission on the Space Shuttle
      Challenger Accident, https://history.nasa.gov/rogersrep/v1ch6.htm.

26   This exercise is a component of the Organization & Relationship
      Systems Coaching™ curriculum. Copyright © 2015 CRR Global. All
      rights reserved.

27   Amy Edmondson, "Building a Psychologically Safe Workplace," TED
      video.

28   Amy Edmondson, *Teaming: How Organizations Learn, Innovate, and
      Compete in the Knowledge Economy* (San Francisco, CA: Jossey-Bass
      Pfeifer, 2014).

29   Paul J. Zak, "The Neuroscience of Trust," *Harvard Business Review*, January–February 2017, https://hbr.org/product/the-neuroscience-of-trust/R1701E-PDF-ENG.

30   Paul J. Zak, "Trust and Growth," *Economic Journal* 111, no. 470 (2001): 295–321, https://econpapers.repec.org/RePEc:ecj:econjl:v:111:y:2001:i:470:p:295-321.

31   Paul J. Zak, "The Neuroscience of Trust," *Harvard Business Review*, January–February 2017, https://hbr.org/product/the-neuroscience-of-trust/R1701E-PDF-ENG.

32   "The Neurobiology of Collective Action," *Front Neurosci*. 7 (November 19, 2013): 211, doi: 10.3389/fnins.2013.00211.

33   David Garvin, "How Google Sold Its Engineers on Management," *Harvard Business Review*, December 2013, https://hbr.org/2013/12/how-google-sold-its-engineers-on-management.

34   Edgar Schein, *Organizational Culture and Leadership*, 4th ed. (San Francisco, CA: Jossey Bass, 2010).

35   The CultureTalk Survey was developed by Cynthia Forstmann, Theresa Agresta and Andrea Cotter, co-founders of CultureTalk. Information about the survey can be found at www.culturetalk.com

36   Edgar Schein, *Organizational Culture and Leadership*, 4th ed. (San Francisco: CA: Jossey Bass, 2010).

37   Ibid.

38   Ibid.

Chapter Four

39   William Bridges, *Transitions: Making Sense of Life's Changes* (Cambridge, MA: Da Capo Lifelong Books, 2004).

40   Dr. Diana Whitney, "Appreciative Inquiry: A Positive Revolution in Change," in *The Change Handbook*, ed. Peggy Holman, Tom Devane, and Steven Cady (San Francisco, CA: Berrett-Koehler Publishers, Inc., 2006), www.academia.edu/4063158/Appreciative_Inquiry_A_Positive_Revolution_in_Change.

41   Carol Dweck, "What Having a 'Growth Mindset' Actually Means," *Harvard Business Review*, January 13, 2016, https://hbr.org/product/what-having-a-growth-mindset-actually-means/H02LQX-PDF-ENG.

42   Steve Chandler, *Crazy Good* (Anna Maria, FL: Maurice Bassett, 2015).

Chapter Five

43   William Bridges, *Transitions: Making Sense of Life's Changes* (Cambridge, MA: Da Capo Lifelong Books, 2004).

44   While this use of the term has become increasingly more common, one of the leaders in helping to bring the concept to the forefront of herbal medicine is David Winston and Steven Maimes, *Adaptogens: Herbs for Strength, Stamina, and Stress Relief* (Rochester, VT: Inner Traditions/Bear & Company, 2007).

45   Vijay Govindarajan and Chris Trimble, *Reverse Innovation: Create Far From Home, Win Everywhere.* (Boston, MA: Harvard Business School Publishing, 2012).

46   Robert Kegan and Lisa Laskew Lahey, *An Everyone Culture: Becoming a Deliberately Developmental Organization* (Boston, MA: Harvard Business Review Press, 2016), 2, https://hbr.org/product/an-everyone-culture-becoming-a-deliberately-developmental-organization/14259-HBK-ENG.

47   Michael Ben-Eli, "Design Science: A Framework for Change" (New York: Buckminster Fuller, 2007), https://issuu.com/buckminster_fuller_institute/docs/designscience.

48   Donella Meadows, *Thinking in Systems: A Primer* (White River Junction, VT: Chelsea Green Publishing, 2008).

49   Michael Mankins. *Time, Talent, Energy* (Boston, MA: Harvard Business Review Press, 2017).

50   Donella Meadows, *Thinking in Systems: A Primer* (White River Junction, VT: Chelsea Green Publishing, 2008).

51   Ibid.

52   Ibid.

53   Ibid.

54   Thomas Kuhn, *The Structure of Scientific Revolutions* (Chicago: University of Chicago Press, 1962).

55   Tim Brown, IDEO CEO. The Design Thinking page of IDEO U. www.ideou.com/pages/design-thinking.

56   W. M. Thorburn, "Occam's Razor," *Mind* 24 (1915): 287–288.

57   Stanford Design School, "I Like, I Wish, What If," Stanford Design School, https://dschool-old.stanford.edu/wp-content/themes/dschool/method-cards/i-like-i-wish-what-if.pdf.

Chapter Six

58   Rikke Dam and Teo Siang of the Interaction Design Foundation and can be found online at www.interaction-design.org/literature/article/design-thinking-get-started-with-prototyping.

59   Janice Sempler interview with Linda Sharkey in 2016. An overview of that conversation can be found at Sharkey's site: http://lindasharkey.com/a-talk-with-janice-semper/.

60   Rikke Dam and Teo Siang of the Interaction Design Foundation and can be found online at www.interaction-design.org/literature/article/design-thinking-get-started-with-prototyping.

61   Tim Brown, *Change by Design: How Design Thinking Transforms Organizations and Inspires Innovation* (New York: HarperCollins, 2009).

62   Stanford Design School, "I Like, I Wish, What If," Stanford Design School, https://dschool-old.stanford.edu/wp-content/themes/dschool/method-cards/i-like-i-wish-what-if.pdf.

63   Seth Godin, "Breakpoints" (blog), May 23, 2016, http://sethgodin.
      typepad.com/seths_blog/2016/05/breakpoints.html.

64   Janice Semper, interview, *Digital Transformation Review*, no.
      10 (2017), https://www.capgemini.com/consulting/resources/
      digital-transformation-review-10/.

65   "Edge" definition and perspective is part of the Organization &
      Relationship Systems CoachingTM curriculum. Copyright © 2015
      CRR Global. All rights reserved.

66   Holocracy refers to a decentralized form of management. Loosely
      defined, decision-making and authority are distributed throughout
      self-organizing teams as opposed to a structure that vests them in a
      traditional management hierarchy.

Chapter Seven

67   William Bridges, *Transitions: Making Sense of Life's Changes*
      (Cambridge, MA: Da Capo Lifelong Books, 2004).

68   Zeal. www.zeal.technology.

Chapter Eight

69   Social Capital definition. Organisation for Economic Co-operation
      and Development (OECD) Available online at https://www.oecd.org/
      insights/37966934.pdf

70   David Zes. Korn Ferry Institute. Available online at https://www.
      kornferry.com/institute/better-return-self-awareness.

71   Ilan Mochari. "How Market Basket's Deposed CEO Earned Employee
      Loyalty" at www.inc.com/ilan-mochari/market-basket-loyalty.html.

Chapter Nine

72   My colleague, Hugh McGill, an organizational change and cultural
      development practitioner, coined this phrase. Hugh's website is www.
      powerful-results.com.

73   Ibid.

74   Learn more about Rajkumary Neogy's work on her website at www.
      disruptivediversity.com/.

Chapter Ten

75   Ibid.

76   Learn more about Rosemary Strunk's work on her website at www.
      living-courageously.com/.

77   Ibid.

34143160R00110

Made in the USA
Middletown, DE
23 January 2019